# PROFILES

## GENERATION ONE - THE TWELVE

**Barry Morrow**

*AuthorHouse™*
*1663 Liberty Drive, Suite 200*
*Bloomington, IN 47403*
*www.authorhouse.com*
*Phone: 1-800-839-8640*

*First published by AuthorHouse  3/4/2008*

*ISBN: 978-1-4343-7022-8 (sc)*

*Library of Congress Control Number: 2008901953*

*Printed in the United States of America*
*Bloomington, Indiana*

*This book is printed on acid-free paper.*

authorHOUSE®

# PROFILES
## GENERATION ONE - THE TWELVE

## Introduction to this Guide

This Life Guide is designed for use in conjunction with the **Generation One** music CD in either group or individual study. In group settings, the Life Guide lends itself favorably to a small group ministry of a church, as well as a sermon series a pastor might devote to the lives of the apostles.

If the Life Guide is used in a small group setting, it will become apparent that the material on each disciple is perhaps more than can be covered in one meeting, so the group leader may want to select what he or she thinks are the most relevant and appropriate questions for the group's discussion.

Similarly, if a pastor chooses to preach a series on the lives of the apostles, although he will want to do his own Biblical studies, he will find a wealth of information in the Life Guide biographical sections on each of the apostles. Again, for the needs and interests of his church, he may choose to tailor his messages to cover key aspects of a disciple's life as it best fits the needs and interests of his church.

For each of the disciples in the Life Guide, a biography of each disciple is given, followed by discussion questions (*Discussion*) which seeks to address different Biblical themes taken from each of the disciple's lives. These questions are then followed by quotes (*Expressions*) from various authors in the Christian tradition that generally relate to the themes previously addressed in the discussion questions. Following the quotes, several Scriptural passages are provided (*Meditations*) for further reflection on each disciple. Each study then closes with an opportunity to prayerfully reflect (*Reflections*) on certain attributes exhibited by that apostle, in terms of gratitude, mindset, and a personal aspiration.

# The Twelve

Over the twenty centuries in the history of Christendom, there has been unending fascination with the twelve chosen disciples of Jesus Christ. How is it that these twelve ordinary men changed the world? They were not known as scholars, nor were many of them gifted with great oratory skills and erudition. Most of the disciples came from Galilee, the northern region of Israel that was known to be a major crossroads for trade routes. An unsophisticated area that often faced the derision and ridicule of the rest of the country, Galilee certainly could not measure up to Jerusalem in Judea, the religious capital of Israel.

And these followers of Christ came from various walks of life. Four, and perhaps as many as seven of the disciples, were fishermen who had probably been lifelong friends from Capernaum, on the north shores of the Sea of Galilee. One was a hated tax collector, employed by the Romans to extort money from his own people. Another, at the opposite end of the political spectrum, was a fiery zealot who wanted to overthrow the Roman government's oppressive rule over Israel. Interestingly, not *one* of the Twelve was a rabbi, priest, scribe, or Pharisee, representing the official religious establishment of Israel!

What is remarkable is that Jesus' entire earthly ministry, from His baptism by John the Baptist to His resurrection, lasted only around three years. A. B. Bruce, in his classic work, *The Training of the Twelve*, has observed that by the time Christ had identified and called the Twelve from a larger group of followers (Matthew 10:1-4, Luke 6:12-16), *half* of His earthly ministry was already over!

A.B. Bruce writes:

*"The selection by Jesus of the Twelve...is an important landmark in the Gospel history. It divides the ministry of our Lord into two portions, nearly equal, probably, as to duration, but unequal as to the extent and importance of the work done in each respectively. In the earlier period Jesus labored single-handed; His miraculous deeds were confined for the most part to a limited area, and His teaching was in the main of an elementary character. But by the time when the twelve were chosen, the work of the kingdom had assumed such dimensions as to require organization and division of labor; and the teaching of Jesus was beginning to be of a deeper and more elaborate nature, and His gracious activities were taking on an ever-widening range. It is probable that the selection of a limited number to be His close and constant companions had become a necessity to Christ, in consequence of His very success in gaining disciples. His followers, we imagine, had grown so numerous as to be an encumbrance and an impediment to his movements..."*

Simply put, this means that these twelve men, whose backgrounds were largely in mundane trades, had little more than eighteen months for the training of the monumental task with which they were entrusted. There was no Plan B if the Twelve should fail. The strategy by Jesus seems risky to say the least, yet Christ obviously knew what He was doing. He realized that the ultimate success of the Twelve would be guided by the Holy Spirit, who would lead these ordinary men to accomplish His sovereign purposes.

In the New Testament, the Twelve are sometimes referred to by the general term, "disciples" (from the Greek word, *mathetes*), which means "learner" (Matthew 10:1, 11:1, 20:17, Luke 9:1), but they are also referred to by the term, "apostles," (from the Greek word, *apostello*), which essentially means, "sent ones." This latter title takes on a technical meaning in the New Testament, and is frequently employed by Luke in his two works, the Gospel of Luke and the Book of Acts, to refer exclusively to the Twelve. Interestingly, the Gospel writers Matthew, Mark, and John, use the term "apostle" sparingly, preferring to refer to the disciples by the term, "the twelve" (Matthew 11:1, Mark 3:14, John 6:67).

Because of their unique calling and office to which the Twelve were called, their role was foundational to the Christian Church. As such, they were occasionally entrusted with supernatural powers to authenticate the truth of the Gospel, which they had received from Christ, and for which they served as ambassadors after His departure (Ephesians 2:20, Matthew 10:1, Luke 9:1-2, Acts 2:3-4, Hebrews 2:3-4). While our attention is focused on the Twelve, who shared Jesus' public ministry with Him, it should also be noted that the apostle Paul was also considered an apostle, although his conversion did not occur until *after* Christ's ascension (Acts 9). Paul's epistles clearly demonstrate that he was similarly called to fill a special "apostolic" office, that of "apostle to the Gentiles" (Romans 11:13, 1 Timothy 2:7, 2 Timothy 1:11, 2 Corinthians 11:5), and that he was recognized as having similar authority (2 Peter 3:15-16).

In Christ's choosing of the Twelve, it is sometimes imagined that His call was a simplistic, "Follow Me," as though He simply said the word, and they blindly followed. But a closer reading of Scripture gives us a more accurate perspective that His call to the Twelve was actually in various stages. Some have observed that the call of five of the disciples in John 1:35-51, as they encountered Jesus for the first time, was a call to *conversion*. A second phase of their calling is seen in Luke 5, centered around Jesus' miraculous provision of fish for these fishermen, at which time they left all and followed Him (Matthew 4:19-22, Luke 5:11). This was their call to *ministry*. Yet a third aspect of their calling was a call to *apostleship*, at which time Christ selected and appointed these men to be His apostles during the latter half of His three year ministry (Matthew 10:1-4, Luke 6:12-16). This apostleship phase was essentially the "on the job training," where the disciples would be instructed by Christ, and then sent out often, two by two, to offer mutual support to each other. They would always be checking back with Him, to let Him know of the challenges they faced (Luke 9:10, 10:17). Then, after a few periods of evangelistic labors, they would return to the Lord and remain with Him for more teaching, fellowship, and rest (Mark 6:30-34). A final, fourth phase of their calling occurred *after* Jesus' crucifixion and resurrection, when He appeared to the Twelve, and others, for a period of forty days before His ascension in heaven (Acts 1:1-4, 1 Corinthians 15:1-5). During this time, He was involved with the Twelve in further teaching them, and spending time with them, before He sent them out into the world with His message of redemption for the world (Acts 1:8). This fourth phase might be referred to as a calling to *martyrdom*.

Significantly, each of these men, for all of their frailties, flaws and unbelief during Jesus' earthly ministry, would ultimately give their life for the sake of the Gospel. History and tradition records that all but one of the Twelve were martyred – only the apostle John is said to have lived to an old age (exiled on the island of Patmos), and still he was greatly persecuted for his testimony about Christ (John 21, Revelation 1).

Despite the obstacles that these men faced, and their human weaknesses (they were a lot like us), they triumphed! Even in the midst of severe persecution, and eventual martyrdom, they fulfilled Christ's calling in their lives, and their continuing witness over the past two thousand years is reason enough to find continual interest and fascination with their lives, as well as a faith worth following in the twenty-first century.

A fitting epitaph for the Twelve, who gave their lives for the Gospel, was uttered by Jim Eliot a half a century ago. A Christian missionary to the Auca Indians, Eliot, along with his companions, was martyred by the very people to whom he was bringing the Gospel. Eliot observed:

*"He is no fool who gives up what he cannot keep, to gain what he cannot lose."*

# John
## *The Wonder of Love*
### **The Power of Love To Transform a Life**

Apart from the Apostle Paul and Luke the physician (who wrote his Gospel and the Acts of the Apostles) John records the most of any other writer of the New Testament. From his own Gospel we get a provocative portrait of Jesus Christ, quite distinct from the other three Gospels, as over ninety percent of his material occurs no where else in the New Testament. His gospel is often referred to as the "philosopher's gospel," because of his deep and brooding thinking. Historian Philip Schaff described John as "a man of mystic contemplation…simple, serene, profound, intuitive, and sublime." Apart from his gospel, his three epistles describe how he dealt with the churches in what is today modern Turkey. And from the book of Revelation, which he received from Christ during his exile on the island of Patmos, we get a glimpse of the future, apocalyptic destiny of our world.

As we consider the various passages of the New Testament, we are able to piece together a good deal about John. We know that he was the younger brother of James, and they are referred to as the "sons of Zebedee." Their father was probably a wealthy businessman who had a fishing business, (Mark 1:20), and their mother Salome, many consider was the sister of Mary, the mother of Jesus. Because John was known to the high priest at the time of Jesus' arrest (John 18:15-16), some have suggested that his family was a prominent family in Jerusalem, with his father perhaps a Levite, and so related to the family of the high priest.

While the New Testament suggests that John's role was not initially a dominant one in the early church (he seems to be secondary to Peter in Acts 1-12), it is frequently pointed out that he was the disciple closest to Christ. And while his older brother James would be the first disciple martyred for his faith (Acts 12:2), John is the last disciple to die, tradition holds, of old age at the end of the first century, and the only disciple not to die a martyr's death (John 21).

What is abundantly clear from the New Testament is that John was one of three disciples who were considered part of Jesus' inner circle of faithful confidants. It is only the apostle John, along with his brother James and Peter, who are permitted to be in Jesus' company when he raised Jairus' daughter from the dead (Mark 5:37); it is only these three disciples who are given the privilege to see Jesus' Transfiguration, where He is accompanied by Moses and Elijah on a high mountain in Israel (Matthew 17:1ff.); and lastly, only these three disciples were invited by Jesus to accompany Him as He retreated in prayer in the Garden of Gethsemane on the evening of His betrayal (Mark 14:33).

While John is often referred to as the "Apostle of Love," it is clear that early on, he and his older brother James had passionate, fiery temperaments. It should not be overlooked that Jesus nicknamed these two brothers, "Sons of *Boanerges*," meaning "Sons of Thunder" (Mark 3:17). Three passages in particular display the fiery temperament of John. The first passage is Mark 9:38-40, which is also the only place in the New Testament where John appears and speaks by himself. Ironically, this passage comes on the heels of the Transfiguration at the beginning of Mark 9, after which the inner circle of the disciples (Peter, James, and John), feeling a sense of superiority, led to the disciples' debate as to who was the greatest among them (Mark 9:33ff.). Then we read in Mark 9:38ff., "John said to Jesus, 'Teacher, we saw a man using your name to cast out demons, but we told him to stop because he isn't one of our group." To which Jesus replied: "Don't stop him! No one who performs miracles in My name will soon be able to speak evil of Me. Anyone who is not against us is for us" (Mark 9:39-40). Clearly, John expresses an elitist, arrogant attitude, believing that anyone outside the circle of Jesus' chosen disciples is not worthy of ministry on His behalf, even when they perform it in Jesus' name! The Old Testament parallel to this incident is found in Numbers 11:26-30, where Joshua pleads with Moses to hinder the prophetic work of two prophets who are not considered as having the proper "credentials" to minister prophetically apart from Moses.

A second passage that exhibits the fiery temperament of John and his brother James is in Luke 9, when Jesus and His disciples are journeying toward Jerusalem, and Jesus sends messengers ahead to a Samaritan village to prepare for His arrival. When these messengers are refused, because they don't want to have any dealings with Jesus and His disciples, James and John, upon hearing of this, asked Jesus: "Lord, should we order down fire from heaven to burn them up? But Jesus turned and rebuked them. So they went on to another village" (Luke 9: 54-56). The two Sons of Thunder believed they were on solid footing, reminiscent of the Old Testament prophet Elijah, who called down fire from heaven (2 Kings 1). Yet Jesus would show them another way, the way of mercy, not judgment.

Yet another passage where we see the ambitious, driven temperaments of both John and James is in Mark 10, where these Sons of Thunder ask of Jesus a favor. We read in verse 35 and following: "James and John, the sons of Zebedee, came over and spoke to him, 'Teacher,' they said, 'we want you to do us a favor.' 'What is it?' He asked. 'In your glorious kingdom, we want to sit in places of honor next to you,' they said, 'one at your right and the other at your left.' But Jesus answered, 'You don't know what you are asking! Are you able to drink from the bitter cup of sorrow I am about to drink? Are you able to be baptized with the baptism of suffering I must be baptized with?' 'Oh yes, we are able!' they said." The sons of Zebedee did not understand the sufferings Jesus must endure to fulfill God's plan of redemption. Also, it is interesting to note that in the parallel passage of this event, Matthew 20:20ff., James and John seem to have enlisted their mother to make this request of Jesus, that her sons have the places of honor when His kingdom comes. One can understand why the other ten disciples became indignant of such an audacious request (Matthew 20:24), and Jesus, always the Teacher *par excellence*, never missed an opportunity to teach the disciples about true servanthood (Matthew 20: 25-28).

As seen from these examples, John had a passionate disposition, yet it is also true that he had a passion for the truth. Of all the New Testament writers, John tends to live in a world of black and white, with very little gray. His is the world of Light and Darkness, of Life and Death, of the Kingdom of God and the Kingdom of Satan. John will use the common Greek work for "truth," (*aletheia*), over forty-five times in his Gospel and his epistles, more than any other New Testament writer. To John, there is little in between – he doesn't know the meaning of the word "compromise." And while John knows that

Christians will sin (1 John 1: 8, 10, 2:1), he does not dwell upon that point so much as to suggest that the pattern of new life in Christ focuses on righteousness as the dominant "rhythm" of the Christian's life. To read John, and John alone, we might come away with the idea that Christian spirituality comes easily, naturally, and yet we know this is not so. To get a proper Biblical balance between the Black-and-White of John, and the rest of the New Testament, we must read the Apostle Paul, the Apostle of Exceptions, who speaks of the difficulties and challenges of living a life of righteousness (Romans 7:14ff., 12: 1-2, Galatians 5:16ff.) Perhaps this Black-and-White temperament helps to explain (not excuse) much of John's seemingly prideful and ambitious vignettes we see from his writings in the New Testament.

And yet, for all the pride, sectarianism, and ambition that characterized John (and his brother James) in his dealings with the disciples and others, this is not the whole story. The "rest of the story" is that the Apostle John aged well. True, his natural temperament made him prone to excesses and pride, and yet, in later life he received the epithet, "apostle of love." True, his world was dominated by his passion for truth, as we have already seen, but we see in his Gospel and his epistles also the emphasis on love, by his use of the common Greek word *agape*, which occurs over eighty times in his writings.

John would come to understand, as he witnessed the sufferings of Christ (he may have been the only disciple who was an eye-witness of Christ's crucifixion, John 19:26), that greatness is measured not by attitudes of superiority, but by acts of servanthood. John, with the rest of the disciples, perhaps only began to grasp this idea of servanthood on the night Jesus was betrayed, when in the upper room with the twelve disciples, He washed the disciples' feet, and as has been said, "redefined greatness" (John 13:1-17).

It has often been observed that while the Gospel of John was written by John, the brother of James, the son of Zebedee, nowhere in the Gospel does he identify himself by name. He refers to himself simply as "the disciple whom Jesus loved" (John 13:23, 20:2, 21:7, 20). Here was the disciple who had the seat of honor at the Last Supper (John 13:23), and who was given the responsibility of caring for Mary, Jesus' mother, after His crucifixion (John 19:26-27), and yet he never refers to himself by name. Why? It may very well be that his years of ambition and self-promotion had been tempered by Jesus' sacrifice, and consequently, he desired no longer to bring any attention to himself, but only to Jesus Christ.

Tradition suggests that John became the pastor of the church in Ephesus that was founded by the Apostle Paul. And later, because of his testimony concerning Jesus Christ, he was exiled to the island of Patmos in the Aegean Sea, during a great persecution of the church under the Roman Emperor Domitian (Revelation 1:9). Furthermore, tradition holds (and John 21:21-23 might suggest this) that while all the disciples faced a martyr's death, John died of old age, probably around A.D. 98, under the reign of the Roman Emperor Trajan.

Jerome, an early Church Father, tells an interesting story in his commentary on the New Testament book of Galatians. Supposedly when John was old and frail, unable to walk, his disciples would carry him in to church. And he would always greet his disciples with the phrase, "My little children, love one another." Being a bit exasperated by this often-heard phrase from the aged apostle, his disciples asked him, "Why do you *always* give us this commandment?" To which John is reported to have said, "It is the Lord's commandment. And if this alone be done, it is enough!"

Through Christ's life and teachings, John had his world turned upside down as he witnessed a revolution like no other, of a kingdom born not of justice, but of grace. Formerly one of the "Sons of Thunder," when John decided to let love have its way with him, he would come to be known in history as the "Apostle of Love," because of the wonder of the Savior's love. And like the Apostle John, when we come face to face with His unimagined grace, we are granted the privilege to live in awe of the power that not only can have its way with us, but also will one day rule the world.

# DISCUSSION

*THE INNER CIRCLE*

One of the most telling passages involving John is found in Mark 9, which is the only occurrence in the New Testament where John appears and speaks by himself. We read in Mark 9:38ff., "John said to Jesus, 'Teacher, we saw a man using your name to cast out demons, but we told him to stop because he isn't one of our group." To which Jesus replied: "Don't stop him! No one who performs miracles in My name will soon be able to speak evil of Me. Anyone who is not against us is for us" (Mark 9:39-40). As you examine this passage, what occurred earlier in the chapter that may have led to John asking this question of Jesus?

What do you think Jesus was trying to get across to John and the disciples by His response?

*RELIGIOUS AMBITION NOTHING NEW*

There is a parallel incident to the Mark 9 passage that is found in the Old Testament in Numbers 11:26-30, where Joshua pleads with Moses to stop the ministry of two prophets. As you read this passage, what are the significant parallels between these two stories?

A similar spirit is exhibited by James and John in Luke 9: 54-56, when they ask Jesus if they can call down fire from Heaven to destroy a Samaritan village that refused Jesus and the disciples hospitality (see also 2 Kings 1). What lessons are we to learn from these passages about the challenges of ministry?

What are some of the dangers of spiritual leadership and authority?

*SO GOD HAS FAVORITES?*

Throughout his Gospel, John never identifies himself by name, but only as "the disciple whom Jesus loved" (John 13:23, 20:2, 21:7, 20). Why do you think he referred to himself this way?

Are we to conclude that John was *more loved* than the rest of the disciples?

So does God have "favorites"?

Although John was known as the "Apostle of Love," he also had a fiery disposition and a passion for the truth. His world was a world of Light and Darkness, of Life and Death, the Kingdom of God battling the Kingdom of Satan. He didn't know how to spell the word "compromise"! Check out John's words in his first letter, 1 John 2:15-17. What is he saying in these verses?

What are some areas of life where you believe Christians are most challenged to compromise their faith?

What influences us to compromise our values?

What are a few areas that you are most challenged in living for Christ in the world?

# EXPRESSIONS

*"Who is the greatest in the kingdom of Heaven? The disciples asked this because they were trying hard, and Jesus showed them a child who in all probability neither knew nor much cared to know what the kingdom of Heaven was nor what such a question might mean. And then He told them to become like that little child—neither knowing in the sense of understanding nor caring in the sense of being anxious."*

-Frederick Buechner, *The Magnificent Defeat*

*"The most difficult lie I have ever contended with is this: Life is a story about me. God brought me to Graceland to rid me of this deception, to scrub it out of the gray matter of my mind. It was a frustrating and painful experience. I hear addicts talk about the shakes and panic attacks and the highs and lows of resisting their habit, and to some degree I understand them because I have had habits of my own, but no drug is so powerful as the drug of self. No rut in the mind is so deep as the one that says I am the world, the world belongs to me, all people are characters in my play. There is not addiction so powerful as self-addiction."*

–Donald Miller, *Blue Like Jazz: Nonreligious Thoughts on Christian Spirituality*

*"There is one vice of which no man in the world is free; which every one on the world loathes when he sees it in someone else; and of which hardly any people, except Christians, ever imagine that they are guilty themselves…The vice I am talking about is Pride or Self-Conceit…Well, now we have come to the centre…Pride leads to every other vice: it is the complete anti-God state of mind…if you want to find out how proud you are the easiest way is to ask yourself, 'How much do I dislike it when other people snub me, or refuse to take any notice of me, or shove their oar in, or patronize me, or show off?' The point is that each person's pride is in competition with every one else's pride. It is because I wanted to be the big noise at the party that I am so annoyed at someone else being the big noise…It is the comparison that makes you proud: the pleasure of being above the rest. Once the element of competition has gone, pride has gone…"*

–C.S. Lewis, "The Great Sin," *Mere Christianity*

# MEDITATIONS

*"And there arose also a dispute among them as to which one of them was regarded to be greatest. And He said to them, 'The kings of the Gentiles lord it over them; and those who have authority over them are called 'Benefactors.' But not so with you, but let him who is the greatest among you become as the youngest, and the leader as the servant."*

–Luke 22:24-26

*"Do not love the world, nor the things of the world. If anyone loves the world, the love of the Father is not in him. For all that is in the world, the lust of the flesh and the lust of the eyes and the boastful pride of life, is not from the Father, but is from the world. And the world is passing away, and also its lusts; but the one who does the will of God abides forever."*

-1 John 2:15-17

# REFLECTIONS

MAY I ALWAYS BE GRATEFUL…that God has dealt with me according to His mercy and grace, rather than according to my deeds.

MAY I ALWAYS BE MINDFUL…that greatness in the eyes of God is measured by my serving others, and not by my success as measured by the external standards of the world.

MAY I ALWAYS BE HOPEFUL…that the wonder of God's love, and His unimaginable grace, will penetrate the hearts and minds of my family and friends who do not know Him.

# Peter
*Believe*
### *Sifted Like Wheat*

Simon Peter was a fisherman by trade, and he and his brother Andrew were part of a family fishing business based on the northern shores of the Sea of Galilee in the town of Capernaum. We know that in Jesus' day, Capernaum was the primary town on the north tip of the Sea of Galilee, and Jesus during His earthly ministry made Capernaum His home and the base of His ministry for a number of months. Peter and Andrew's home may very well have served as Jesus' primary residence during His ministry there (Mark 1:29). We also know that Simon Peter had a wife, since Luke reports that Christ healed his mother-in-law (Luke 4:38), and similarly, the Apostle Paul tells us that Peter took along his wife on his missionary endeavors (1 Corinthians 9:5).

In the New Testament we have four different lists of the Apostles (Matthew 10:2-4, Mark 3:16-19, Luke 6:13-16, and Acts 1:13), and in all four lists, the same twelve men are mentioned. Not surprisingly, Peter, the leader among the Twelve, is always listed at the top of the lists (Matthew 10:2). In these lists there appears to be three groupings containing four Apostles, each with the inner circle of disciples (Peter, James, and John) having the preeminent position. It was these three disciples, those closest to Christ, who accompanied Him at three important events: the Transfiguration (Matthew 17:1), the raising of Jairus' daughter (Mark 5:37), and His invitation during His private praying at Gethsemane (Mark 14:35). Indeed, Peter is mentioned in the Gospels more than any other name other than Jesus. Furthermore, no one speaks more often than Peter, no other disciple is spoken to by Christ as often as Peter, and no other disciple is so frequently rebuked by the Lord as Peter. And remarkably – no disciple *ever* rebuked the Lord - except Peter! (Matthew 16:22).

The name "Simon" was a very common name in Israel, as we read of at least seven Simons in the Gospels alone. Even among the Twelve, we have two Simons, Simon Peter and Simon the Zealot (Jesus also had a half-brother who was named Simon, Matthew 13:55). Our Simon, Simon Peter, had the full name, "Simon Bar Jonah" (Matthew 16:17), which means, "Simon, son of Jonah" (John 21:15-17). Yet we also know that the Lord gave Simon another name, "Peter." Interestingly, Luke in his Gospel mentions that the Lord "also named Him Peter" (Luke 6:14). Note that this was not a new name, but an *additional* name, and we sometimes see Peter referred to as Simon, sometimes Peter, and at other times Simon Peter. Simon received this nickname "Peter" in his early encounter with Jesus that is recorded in John 1:42, and the name "Peter" derives from the Greek word *Petros*, which means "rock, piece of stone." Likewise, Peter, "the Rock" is sometimes referred to in the New Testament as *Cephas*, which is the Aramaic equivalent for *Petros* (1 Corinthians 1:12, 3:22, 9:5, 15:5, Galatians 2:9).

Much has been made of Peter's turbulent temperament. He clearly was not a particularly modest man, but was usually self-assertive, standing in the forefront as the spokesman for the apostles. So when we read of Peter in the Gospels, we get the picture that he was a cocky, brash follower of Christ who seemed to always be sticking his foot in his mouth, making great promises of fidelity to Christ (above the other disciples), and yet the one whose walk did not match his talk! It may be significant that sometimes the Lord would refer to him as "Simon," and at other times, "Peter." Some have suggested that when He referred to him as *Simon*, the context generally signaled that Peter was in need of correction or rebuke, but when the name *Peter* was used by Christ, He was commending him for obedience or proper conduct.

Needless to say, the portrait of Peter in the Gospels is that of a complex man. It was Peter who asked more questions of Christ than all the other the disciples: it was Peter who asked Christ to explain His difficult sayings (Matthew 15:15, Luke 12:41); it was Peter who asked how many times he needed to forgive an erring brother (Matthew 18:21); it was Peter who asked what the reward would be for the disciples for having left everything to become Jesus' disciples (Matthew 19:27); it was Peter who asked about the significance of the withered fig tree (Mark 11:21); and it was Peter who asked the risen Christ questions about the destiny of his close companion, the disciple John (John 21:20-22).

No other disciple vowed such strong belief, not only in Christ's deity, but in His power to even control the forces of nature. One of the most memorable occasions of Peter's faith occurred on a night Jesus came to His disciples, walking on the water in the midst of a violent storm, as they were making their way across the Sea of Galilee. The disciples, seeing Jesus approaching, were terrified, thinking they were seeing a ghost. But He spoke to them, "Take courage, it is I; do not be afraid" (Matthew 14:27). Then Peter made his audacious request: "Lord, if it is You, command me to come to You on the water," and He said, 'Come!" And Peter got out of the boat, and walked on the water and came toward Jesus. But seeing the wind, he became frightened, and beginning to sink, he cried out, "Lord, save me!" (Matthew 14: 28-30). Of course, Jesus reached out to rescue Peter, and rebuked him, "You of little faith, why did you doubt?" (Matthew 14:31). While we may want to criticize Peter for his lack of faith, we still should give him credit for his boldness in getting out of the boat in the first place!

In reality, Peter's faith is a lot like ours, a mixture of both belief and unbelief. His was a rare combination of tremendous strength, and regrettable instability. No other disciple is recorded as having confessed Christ more boldly. When Jesus asked His disciples, "Who do men say that I, the Son of Man, am?" (Matthew 16:13), Peter is the one who categorically proclaimed; "You are the Christ, the Son of the living God!" (Matthew 16:16). Ironically, just after Christ had commended Peter for his confession, telling him that His Father in Heaven had revealed this truth to him (Matthew 16:17), only a few short verses later Peter suffered the strongest rebuke we ever encounter of a disciple in the New Testament. After Christ had began telling His disciples that He must go to Jerusalem and suffer at the hands of the religious leaders, and ultimately face death, Peter took Him aside and attempted to correct Him, "Heaven forbid it, Lord! This will never happen to You!" (Matthew 16:22). Jesus then turned to Peter and remarked, "Get behind Me, Satan! You are a stumbling block to Me; for you are not setting your mind on God's interests, but man's" (Matthew 16:23).

Later on, Peter would again fall prey to Satan's temptations on the very night of Jesus' arrest, and would learn of his own human frailty, despite his resolve of loyalty to Christ. After celebrating the Passover meal in the upper room and singing a hymn together, as Jesus and His disciples headed toward the Mount of Olives, Jesus warned the disciples of their pending desertion: "You will all fall away because of Me this night, for it is written, 'I will strike down the shepherd, and the sheep of the flock shall be scattered'" (Matthew 26:31). Yet Peter could not fathom his own desertion of Christ. And after declaring his unswerving loyalty to Christ before all the disciples, that he would never deny Christ, Jesus made this prophetic statement to him: "Simon, Simon, behold, Satan has demanded permission to sift you like wheat; but I have prayed for you, that your faith may not fail; and you, when once you have turned again, strengthen your brothers" (Luke 22:31-32). Then, despite his protestations of loyalty, "Lord, with You I am ready to go both to prison and to death!" (Luke 22:33), Christ reveals to him: "I say to you, Peter, the rooster will not crow today until you have denied three times that you know Me" (Luke 22:34). Later that night, after Jesus is arrested and brought into the high priest's residence, Jesus' pronouncement of Peter's denials would come true. After being accused of being one of Jesus' followers, and his denial, Luke records that "Immediately, while he (Peter) was still speaking, a rooster crowed. The Lord turned and looked at Peter. And Peter remembered the word of the Lord, how He had told him, 'Before a rooster crows today, you will deny Me three times.' And he went out and wept bitterly" (Luke 22:60-62). Peter's disgrace and shame had to have been magnified, since not only had he denied Christ before these people, but because he had boasted so stubbornly about his loyalty.

It has often been observed that there is a remarkable parallel between Peter's denials of Christ and his threefold "restoration" that we find in the last chapter of John's Gospel. After Peter had decided to go fishing, and the other disciples decided to join him, John tells us that they caught nothing after fishing all night. And as dawn was breaking, Jesus stood on the beach, yet the disciples did not recognize the man as being Jesus (John 21:4). This was the third appearance to the disciples since His bodily resurrection (John 21:14). Jesus asked them: "Children, you do not have any fish, do you?" They answered, "No." And when He had instructed them to cast their nets on the right side of the boat, they found such a catch that they were not able to haul it in! (John 21:6). When the disciple John witnessed this miracle, he told Peter, "It is the Lord!" And when Peter heard these words, he threw himself into the sea and headed for the beach where Christ was, leaving the other disciples to bring in the net brimming with fish (John tells us that the catch was one hundred and fifty-three large fish, yet the net was not torn – clearly an eyewitness account, John 21:11). So Jesus invited the disciples to bring some of the fish they had caught, and join Him for breakfast, yet none of these disciples ventured to ask Him who He was, "for they all knew that it was the Lord" (John 21:13).

Then, after breakfast, as they sat beside the charcoal fire where the fish had been cooked (Peter's earlier denials had *also* been by a charcoal fire as he warmed himself outside the court of the high priest, John 18: 18, 25), Jesus had the following exchange with Peter: "Simon, son of John, do you love Me more than these?" And he said to Him, "Yes, Lord, You know that I love You." And Christ said to him, "Tend My lambs." Then Christ said to Peter a *second* time, "Simon, son of John, do you love Me?" and Peter responded, "Yes, Lord, You know that I love You." And Christ responded, "Shepherd My sheep." Jesus then asked Peter a *third* time, "Simon, son of John, do you love Me?" Peter, grieved that the Lord had asked him the same question three times, responded, "Lord, You know all things. You know that I love You." And Jesus said to him, "Tend My sheep" (John 21: 15-17).

In this remarkable passage, one question that surfaces is whether, when Jesus asked Peter if he loved Him "more than *these*" (verse 15), was Christ referring to Peter loving Christ more than the *other* disciples? Or could He have been asking Peter if he loved Him more than *fishing*? While both interpretations are possible, it seems most likely that Christ was referring to the *other disciples*, since Peter had often pledged his unfailing loyalty to Christ over the others.

A second question that often arises is *why* Christ asks Peter three times whether he loves Him. Many make the point that two different Greek words for "love" are used in Christ's questioning of Peter, and Peter's response only includes one of these words. Christ in His first two questions uses the word for love, *agapao*, which carries the idea of "self-giving, unconditional" love. In contrast, Peter's responses to Christ's threefold question (and Christ's third questioning) uses the word for love, *phileo*, which is more akin to our idea of "like, fond affection" (This Greek word is the root word for which we get "Phila-delphia," city of "brotherly love"). While the significance of these words in Christ's questioning of Peter is debated, perhaps the most important conclusion that we can make is that Christ was using this occasion, with the threefold affirmation from Peter of his love for Christ, to *restore* Peter from his earlier threefold denial.

Despite Peter's many failures, perhaps the greatest redemptive factor of his character was his amazing sense of sin, and tenderness of heart. It was Peter who had said, after being told by Christ where to cast his nets early on, "Depart from me, O Lord, for I am a sinful man" (Luke 5:8). In some respects, Peter's sin was as grievous as Judas', except that Peter repented and Judas did not.

Peter, the leader of this band of motley disciples, with all the brashness and instincts of a natural-born leader, had to be molded and refashioned by Christ for him to be useful to the Master. For all his protestations of loyalty and fidelity *above* his fellow disciples, he had to learn the hard lesson of his own inadequacy, that pride comes before fall, that "let him who thinks he stands take heed that he does not fall" (1 Corinthians 10:12). After Christ's crucifixion and resurrection, and when the Church was birthed at Pentecost (Acts 2), we see a *transformed* Peter in the early church. Three thousand people believed in Christ when he preached at Pentecost (Acts 2:14-41); he and John healed a lame man early on in their ministry (Acts 3:1-10); he raised Dorcas from the dead (Acts 9:36-42); he introduced the Gospel to the Gentiles (Acts 10).

Peter and the other disciples, who had faltered before Christ's crucifixion, now had a renewed passion with the life-changing message of Christ. When he and John were brought before the Sanhedrin, the Jewish ruling counsel, they were forbidden from "speaking in the name of Jesus" (Acts 4:18). Yet they both replied, "Whether it is right in the sight of God to give heed to you rather than to God, you be the judge; for we cannot stop speaking about what we have seen and heard" (Acts 4:19-20).

For the remainder of his life, Peter, recognizing his own frailty, had a renewed appreciation for people who struggled with temptations. Having been sifted by Satan, having recognized the superficiality of his earlier, "untested" faith, he now was able to empathize with others' weaknesses. Years later, reflecting on his own life experiences, and wanting to give encouragement to fellow Christians, he wrote in his first epistle:

*"Humble yourselves under the mighty hand of God, that He may exalt you at the proper time, casting all your anxiety on Him, because He cares for you. Be of sober spirit, be on the alert. Your adversary, the devil, prowls around like a roaring lion, seeking someone to devour. But resist him, firm in your faith, knowing that the same experiences of suffering are being accomplished by your brethren who are in the world. After you have suffered for a little while, the God of all grace, who called you to His eternal glory in Christ, will Himself perfect, confirm, strengthen, and establish you. To Him be dominion forever and ever. Amen"* (1 Peter 5:6-11).

So what became of Peter? We do know that following his threefold restoration by Christ that is described in John 21, he was informed by Christ that he would face a martyr's death: "Truly, truly, I say to you, when you were younger, you used to gird yourself and walk wherever you wished; but when you grow old, you will stretch out your hands and someone else will gird you, and bring you where you do not wish to go.' Now this He said, signifying by what kind of death he would glorify God" (John 21:18-19). While the Scriptures do not give us any details of Peter's death, early church tradition suggests that he was crucified in Rome, probably by the Roman Emperor Nero, about A.D. 69.

Eusebius, in his *Ecclesiastical History*, cites the testimony of Clement, who observed that before Peter was crucified, he was forced to watch the crucifixion of his own wife. And as he watched her being led to her death, Clement says Peter remarked to her, "Remember the Lord." When it came his turn to face crucifixion, he requested that he be crucified upside down, because he wasn't worthy to die as his Lord had died.

Peter had found it incomprehensible that he could deny His Master. He had wanted to believe he could walk on water, to believe that mountains could be moved, and to be strong enough to stand in the face of life's storms. But through his denial of Jesus he learned the painful lesson that his faith, which he thought was so great, looking back, had been small. The impetuous, cocky Simon, whom Jesus early on in His ministry had nicknamed, "The Rock," through his testing and failures, finally became the Rock, and in many ways, the Rock of the early Church. Having recognized his shallow belief before his transformation, he came to understand that Christ Himself could sustain him. And we, like Peter, may think ourselves invincible. But it is through our failures and shortcomings that we realize that we, too, need the grace of God to carry on.

## DISCUSSION

*NO ONE LIKE PETER*

The Apostle Peter's name is mentioned more than any other in the New Testament other than Jesus Christ. Further, none of the other disciples are recorded as having spoken more frequently than Peter, nor were they spoken to by Christ than Peter. And certainly none rebuked Jesus other than Peter! (Matthew 16:22) The picture we have of him in the Gospels is that of a complex man, given to excessive highs and lows. Yet, he was clearly the leader of this band of twelve disciples. Why do you think Christ chose him to be the leader of the Twelve?

*FAITH AND DOUBT*

One of the most remarkable episodes of the New Testament describes Jesus walking on the Sea of Galilee, in the midst of a violent storm, and approaching the disciples, who are crossing the sea in a boat (Matthew 14:22ff.). Peter asks Jesus if he can join the Lord walking on the water, and proceeds to get out of the boat, walking on the water toward Jesus. Then becoming afraid, and beginning to sink, he cries out, "Lord, save me!" Do you think it really happened? Why or why not?

Do you think it is fair to say that Peter's faith was a mixture of both belief and unbelief? Why or why not?

If so, how do you see this pattern being played out in your own life? What are the things that make us lose faith?

*SIFTED LIKE WHEAT*

On the night Jesus was betrayed, despite Peter's grand protestation of loyalty to Christ (despite Jesus' warning that His disciples would desert Him, Matthew 26:31), Jesus said to Peter: "Simon, Simon, behold, Satan has asked to sift you like wheat, but I have prayed for you, that your faith may not fail. And when you have turned back, strengthen your brothers." (Luke 22:31-32) When Peter protests that he is ready to go to prison for Jesus, or even face death (verse 34), Jesus tells him, "Before the rooster crows today, you will deny that you know Me three times." (Luke 22:34). Sadly, this would come to pass shortly, and Peter would go out from the courtyard and weep bitterly (Luke 22:54-62). What do you think Peter learned about himself from this experience?

Many have observed a parallel between Peter's betrayal and Jesus' conversation with him in John 21:15-17. As you read this passage, what do you think is going on in this exchange between Peter and Christ?

Why does Christ ask him *three* times whether he loves Him?

Is Christ trying to make him feel ashamed, or could it be something else?

*FRAIL AS DUST*

Through his own testing and failures with Christ, Peter seems to have recognized his own frailty, and acquired a renewed sense of appreciation for people who struggle with sin and temptation.
Look at his words penned late in his life in his first letter, 1 Peter 5:6-9. How do these words perhaps look back on his trials and tests?

If we are generally "good, virtuous people," what is our challenge in terms of how we view others? How can we guard against this?

What are some of the areas of personal failure that you've experienced that have given you a greater empathy for others during their struggles?

# EXPRESSIONS

*"It is not as a child that I believe and confess Jesus Christ. My hosanna is born of a furnace of doubt."*
-Fyodor Dostoevsky

*"I love to give charity, but I don't want to be charity. This is why I have so much trouble with grace. A few years ago I was listing prayer requests to a friend. As I listed my requests, I mentioned many of my friends and family but never spoke about my personal problems. My friend candidly asked me to reveal my own struggles, but I told him no, that my problems weren't that bad. My friend answered quickly, in the voice of a confident teacher, 'Don, you are not about the charity of God.' In that instant he revealed my motives were not noble, they were prideful…As I drove over the mountain that afternoon, realizing I was too proud to receive God's grace, I was humbled. Who am I to think myself above God's charity? And why would I forsake the riches of God's righteousness for the dung of my own ego?*
–Donald Miller, *Blue Like Jazz: Nonreligious Thoughts on Christian Spirituality*

*"On the whole, God's love for us is a much safer subject to think about than our love for Him. Nobody can always have devout feelings: and even if we could, feelings are not what God principally cares about. Christian Love, either towards God or towards man, is an affair of the will. If we are trying to do His will we are obeying the commandments, 'Thou shalt love the Lord thy God.' He will give us feelings of love if He pleases. We cannot create them for ourselves, and we must not demand them as a right. But the great thing to remember is that, though our feelings come and go, His love for us does not. It is not wearied by our sins, or our indifference; and, therefore, it is quite relentless in its determination that we shall be cured of those sins, at whatever cost to us, at whatever cost to Him."*
–C. S. Lewis, *Mere Christianity*

## MEDITATIONS

*"Brothers, if someone is caught in a sin, you who are spiritual should restore him gently. But watch yourself, or you also may be tempted. Carry each other's burdens, and in this way you will fulfill the law of Christ. If anyone thinks he is something when he is nothing,, he deceives himself."*

–Galatians 6:1-3

*"Humble yourselves under the mighty hand of God, that He may exalt you at the proper time, casting all your anxiety on Him, because He cares for you. Be of sober spirit, be on the alert. Your adversary, the devil, prowls around like a roaring lion, seeking someone to devour. But resist him, firm in your faith, knowing that the same experiences of suffering are being accomplished by your brethren who are in the world. After you have suffered for a little while, the God of all grace, who called you to His eternal glory in Christ, will Himself perfect, confirm, strengthen, and establish you. To Him be dominion forever and ever. Amen"*

–1 Peter 5:6-11

## REFLECTIONS

MAY I ALWAYS BE GRATEFUL…that God's acceptance of me is not based on my performance, but His mercy and grace.

MAY I ALWAYS BE MINDFUL…that any good I do comes from Christ living out His life through me.

MAY I ALWAYS BE HOPEFUL…that as I consider the unfailing love of God in my own life, I would exercise greater faith in God for all that He brings into my life.

# Simon the Zealot
*Inside Out*
## *A Mercenary Whose Life Was Transformed*

One of the more colorful, yet lesser known of the Twelve, was Simon the Zealot (Luke 6:15, Acts 1:13), also known as "Simon the Cananite" in both Matthew 10:4 and Mark 3:18. However, the word "Cananite" does not refer to the village of Cana, or the land of Canaan, but rather derives from the Hebrew word *qanna*, which means, "to be zealous."

Just as the backgrounds of the various disciples were quite different, their political backgrounds were sometimes totally opposite. While Matthew, sometimes called by his Jewish name Levi (Mark 2:14), was a former tax collector, a rogue hire of the Roman government to extort taxes from his own people, Simon the Zealot was clearly at the other end of the political spectrum. Zealots were an outlaw political party who despised the Romans, and consequently, often took violent measures to overthrow Roman rule.

Josephus, the ancient historian, in his *Antiquities*, described four major political parties among the first century A.D. Jews: The *Pharisees*, the religious fundamentalists of their day; the *Sadducees*, religious liberals who denied the supernatural; the *Essenes*, not mentioned in the Scriptures, but mentioned by both Josephus and Philo as ascetic celibates who lived in the desert (near the Dead Sea, close to the caves of Qumran) and were committed to the study of the Law; and the *Zealots*, political extremists who believed any violent action was warranted to overthrow the Roman occupation.

Unlike the Pharisees, who were willing to compromise their convictions for political reasons, the Zealots were militant outlaws who believed only God Himself had the right to rule over the Jews. They had a secret party of assassins, called *sicarii*—"dagger men" (called as such because of the curved daggers they carried in the folds of their robes)—who would murder Roman politicians and soldiers. At their core, the Zealots believed that they were doing God's will by assassinating Roman soldiers and political leaders who stood in their way. Josephus remarked concerning the Zealots:

*"Of the fourth sect of Jewish philosophy, Judas the Galilean was the author. These men agree in all other things with the Pharisaic notions; but they have an inviolable attachment to liberty, and say that God is to be their only Ruler and Lord. They also do not value dying any kinds of death, nor indeed do they heed the deaths of their relations and friends, nor can any such fear make them call any man lord"* (Antiquities 18:6).

Josephus further mentions a revolt "in Gessius Florus's time," which occurred in A.D. 6, when a group of Zealots waged a rebellion against a Roman census tax. The Zealots' founder was Judas the Galilean, who is mentioned by Josephus. Interestingly, Luke the historian, in his Acts of the Apostles, mentions Judas the Galilean when he cites Gamaliel's words of caution to the religious Council. Gamaliel, a respected Pharisee and teacher of the Law (Acts 5:34), warns the religious Council not to be too quick in their judgment of this new movement of followers of this Rabbi, Jesus, for:

*"Judas of Galilee rose up in the days of the census and drew away some people after him; he too perished, and all those who followed him were scattered. So in the present case, I say to you, stay away from these men and let them alone, for if this plan or action is of men, it will be overthrown, but if it is of God, you will not be able to overthrow them; or else you may even be found fighting against God" (Acts 5:37-39).*

Not only were the Zealots, of whom Simon was a card-carrying member, responsible for this revolt in the early first century A.D., but many historians believe that they may have been responsible for the Roman destruction of Jerusalem in A.D. 70. During the siege by Rome, after Titus Vespasian had surrounded the city and cut off supplies, the Zealots actually began killing other Jews who desired to negotiate with the Romans to end the siege. When Titus saw how dire the situation was, he proceeded to destroy the city, massacring thousands of the Jewish inhabitants, as well as carrying off the treasures in the Jewish Temple.

One can only wonder why Jesus would have chosen such a man as Simon to be one of His chosen Twelve. Clearly, he was a man of strong passions and fierce loyalties. And can anyone doubt that there was a time in his life when he would have happily murdered his fellow disciple, the tax collector Matthew, who stood in the way of his own political party loyalty? Yet in the end, Simon and Matthew would become spiritual brethren, called by the same Master, and called to a higher purpose. One can only be amazed at how the Lord transformed this fiery, revolutionary disciple from attempting to turn the world upside down for Israel, into a devoted follower of Christ, to change the world from the *inside out*.

So what became of Simon the Zealot? Some early sources say that after the destruction of Jerusalem in A.D. 70, Simon carried the Gospel north to the British Isles. While we do not know the specifics of how he died, all accounts suggest he was martyred for preaching the Gospel, possibly with the apostle Thaddaeus in Persia. This "zealot" who was once willing to kill, or be killed, for his political party, had found in Christ a greater cause to commit his life to—the proclamation of salvation to obtain forgiveness and an inner freedom, a freedom not of this world.

As Simon observed Christ, how He exemplified goodness, righteousness, and peace, he came to understand that the purpose of his life was far greater than kingdoms and crowns. Rather, it's about finding the peace and freedom that comes from having our lives transformed, of having our personal world turned "inside out." Do we know someone whom we think stands outside the pale of God's grace? Someone we think is beyond God's forgiveness, and His power to transform their lives? Then think of Simon the Zealot…

# DISCUSSION

*UNLIKELY FRIENDS*

If Matthew represented one end of the political spectrum as a former tax collector (employed by the Romans), and Simon the Zealot represented the other end of the continuum (who despised Roman rule), why would Jesus have possibly chosen these very different types of men to be His followers?

Wouldn't there be a significant downside to having these virtual enemies on His leadership team?

*WHERE DOES A ZEALOT FIT IN?*

Simon likely was a man of strong passions and fierce loyalties. What are some of the ways a man like Simon could be used by God in our own day?

How do you think many religious organizations would view a man like Simon?

*UNITY DESPITE DIVERSITY*

Having a Simon and a Matthew among the Twelve would clearly have represented a challenge. The apostle Paul addresses the issue of diversity in the Body of Christ, the Church, in Romans 12:3-8 and I Corinthians 12:7-26. What are some of the key principles you observe from these two passages relating to the Body of Christ, and how we are to function with others so different than ourselves?

*GROWTH THROUGH CONFLICT*

We can only imagine some of the heated discussions and disagreements between Matthew and Simon the Zealot during their days of following Jesus. Paul's words to the Philippians in Philippians 2:1-11 have some important principles about harmony. What principles do you see in these verses?

Can you think of a time when you had a major "falling out" with another follower of Christ?

How did the two of you handle it? What lessons did you learn from the experience?

Are there some things you would do differently if you could go through it again?


*BEYOND THE REACH OF GOD'S GRACE?*

It is doubtful that anyone could have imagined that Christ would invite a political mercenary like Simon the Zealot to be one of His followers. Have you ever thought of someone whom you thought stood outside the reach of God's grace?


Why do we often make such hasty conclusions?


How is Simon the Zealot's life a good reminder in this regard?

# EXPRESSIONS

*"The Bible tells us to love our neighbors, and also to love our enemies, probably because they are the same people."*

–G.K. Chesterton

*"The heart itself is but a small vessel, yet dragons are there, and also lions. There are poisonous beasts and all the treasures of evil. But there too is God, the angels, the life and the kingdom, the light and the apostles, the heavenly cities and the treasuries of grace—all things are there."*

-Macarius

*"To see myself as a sinner is simple enough, as the Oxford English Dictionary defines a sinner as 'a transgressor against the divine law.' If I care to pay attention, which I usually do not, I can find all too many ways in which I transgress regularly against the great commandment, to love God with all my heart and soul, and my neighbor as myself…I am a sinner, and the Presbyterian church offers me a weekly chance to come clean, and to pray, along with others, what is termed a prayer of confession. But pastors can be so reluctant to use the word 'sin' that in church we end up confessing nothing except our highly developed capacity for denial…At such times I picture God as a wily writing teacher who leans across a table and says, not at all gently, 'Could you possibly be troubled to say what you mean?' It would be refreshing to answer, simply, 'I have sinned.'"*

–Kathleen Norris, "Sinner," *Amazing Grace*

# MEDITATIONS

*"For by the grace given to me I say to every one of you: Do not think of yourself more highly than you ought, but rather think of yourself with sober judgment, in accordance with the measure of faith God has given you. Just as each of us has one body with many members, and these members do not all have the same function, so in Christ we who are many form one body, and each member belongs to all the others. We have different gifts, according to the grace given to us."*

–Romans 12:3-6

*"You have heard that it was said, 'Love your neighbor and hate your enemy.' But I tell you: Love your enemies and pray for those who persecute you, that you may be sons of your Father in heaven. He causes his sun to rise on the evil and the good, and sends rain on the righteous and the unrighteous. If you love those who love you, what reward will you get? Are not even the tax collectors doing that? And if you greet only your brothers, what are you doing more than others? Do not even pagans do that? Be perfect, therefore, as your heavenly Father is perfect."*

–Matthew 5:43-45

# REFLECTIONS

MAY I ALWAYS BE GRATEFUL…that God often chooses people quite different from me to do His work.

MAY I ALWAYS BE MINDFUL…that the work of God is not about turning the world upside down, about kingdoms and crowns, but about changing us from the inside out.

MAY I ALWAYS BE HOPEFUL…that I would not look at the Christian life on a performance basis, but that God would continue to work in my heart to provide genuine peace and freedom.

# Philip
## *Come and See*
### *An Invitation Like No Other*

Philip is the fifth disciple named of each of the four lists of disciples mentioned in the New Testament, and is generally considered the leader of the second tier of disciples. While he plays a relatively small role relative to Peter, Andrew, James, and John, he still emerges as a distinct disciple in his own right.

"Philip" which is a Greek name, meaning "lover of horses," without a doubt also had a Jewish name (as all twelve of the disciples were Jewish); although his Jewish name is never mentioned. He probably came from a Hellenistic Jewish family, as the Greek civilization had spread through the Mediterranean after the fourth century B.C. following the conquests of Alexander the Great.

Philip was from Bethsaida, the same village as Peter and Andrew (John 1:44), and there is good biblical precedent to see Philip, along with Nathanael, and five other of the disciples (Peter, Andrew, Thomas, James, John,) to all be fishermen who were from Galilee, likely life long companions before Jesus called them to be His disciples (John 21:3).

While the Gospel writers Matthew, Mark, and Luke provide no specifics about Philip, John's Gospel gives us a few vignettes of what he was like. What is clear is that he has a very distinct character from the inner circle of Jesus' disciples. In John 6, at the feeding of the five thousand (John 6:10 says there were five thousand *men*, so with additional women and children, the actual number may have been closer to ten thousand people), Philip appears to have been given the task of administration for Jesus and His band of disciples, charged with arranging meals and lodging logistics. Some have suggested he had a dour, negative mindset. So when Jesus asks Philip how they are going to feed this large throng of people, he responds with incredulity, "It would take a small fortune to feed such a multitude!" (John 6:7). John tells us that Jesus was actually testing Philip, for He already knew what He was going to do" (John 6:6).

Later in John, he appears both indecisive, when a group of Greeks wanted to meet with Jesus (John 12:20-21), and thick-headed, as seen in John 14. In the latter passage, as Jesus is meeting with His disciples at the Last Supper in the Upper Room, the last night of His earthly ministry, He is preparing His disciples for his departure. He tells them that He does not want them to be troubled, because He is going to prepare a place for them (John 14:1-2). As the disciples are trying to understand what Jesus is saying, Thomas, probably speaking for all the disciples, asks Him: "Lord, we do not know where You are going, and how can we know the way?" (John 14:5). Jesus makes His famous declaration: "I am the way, the truth, and the life. No one comes to the Father except through Me" (John 14:6). Following Jesus' next statement, where He explicitly claims His deity, Philip speaks up: "Lord, show us the Father, and it is sufficient for us" (John 14:8). Jesus is clearly disappointed by such a question, and chides Philip: "Have I been with you so long, and yet you have not known Me, Philip? He who has seen Me has seen the Father; so how can you say, 'Show us the Father'?" (John 14:9).

Perhaps the most memorable passage about Philip is our initial encounter with him in the first chapter of John's Gospel, the day after Jesus had called Peter, Andrew, and John. Evidently Philip and Nathanael (the disciple also known as Bartholomew), were close friends. And while Peter, Andrew, and John had been encouraged by John the Baptist to follow Jesus as the Messiah, it is Philip who is the *first* disciple actually sought out by Jesus, and invited, "Follow Me" (John 1:43).

Philip, from his study of the Old Testament Scriptures, shows his seeking heart, as well as a passion to make sure his good friend, Nathanael, immediately hears of this good news. John writes of his initial response to Jesus' invitation: "Philip found Nathanael and said to him: 'We have found Him of whom Moses in the Law, and also the Prophets, wrote: Jesus of Nazareth, the son of Joseph'" (John 1:45). While Nathanael is initially unimpressed with Philip's excited discovery ("Nazareth? Can any good thing come out of Nazareth?" John 1:45), Philip was undaunted by his friend's sarcasm: "Come and see!" (John 1:46). Jesus' personal invitation to him to follow Him had a profound impact in his life. When the Messiah gave him this invitation, he must have felt deep down inside that now at last, the peace and purpose of life had now been made clear to him.

Tradition concerning Philip suggests that he was tremendously used in the growth of the early church, and was one of the first apostles to face martyrdom. By most accounts he was stoned to death at Hierapolis, in Phrygia (Asia Minor), some eight years after the martyrdom of James the Great, around A.D. 52 (Acts 12:2).

When Jesus sought out Philip, and invited him to be His disciple, it profoundly changed Philip for the rest of his life. The One who had come and found him, and made His mercy known, now empowered Philip with a significant purpose and plan for his life. He now knew that through Jesus the Messiah, the ultimate Answer had appeared – he could have the peace of forgiveness and the hope of heaven as his true home. And the offer is still made today to you and me, to all those who are willing to seek Him, "Come and see"…

# DISCUSSION

*FIRST ENCOUNTERS*

When we first encounter Philip in the first chapter of John's Gospel, verse 43, we read that as Jesus was leaving for Galilee, He said to Philip, "Follow Me." How was his first encounter with Jesus different from that of John, Andrew, and Simon the day before? (John 1:35-42)

Do you think there is any significance to this?

*SPIRITUAL OBTUSENESS*

One of the most curious exchanges between Jesus and Philip occurs in John 14, part of what is known as Jesus' Upper Room Discourse (John 13-17) given the night He was betrayed. After He makes His famous declaration of deity, "I am the Way, the Truth, and the Life. No one comes to the Father except through Me," John 14:6, Philip says to Him: "Lord, show us the Father and that will be enough for us" (John 14:8). What do you think Philip was asking Jesus?

How do you understand Jesus' response to him in John 14:9ff?

Why didn't Philip "get it"?

Do you think you and I would have been any different? Why or why not?

*BREAD FROM ABOVE*

In another encounter between Philip and Christ in John 6, we read of Jesus' miraculous feeding of the five thousand. When Jesus asks Philip how they are going to feed such a vast multitude, Philip answers: "Eight months wages would not buy enough bread for each one to have a bite!" (John 6:7) As an aside, John tells us that Jesus is actually testing Philip, "for He already had in mind what He was going to do" (John 6:6). If you had been Philip on that occasion, how do you think you would have answered Jesus? Why?

Reflecting on this passage in John 6, do you think it is possible for us to discern when God is going to use "ordinary means" to work His purposes, or "supernatural means"? Why or why not?

Do you think our faith has an influence on how God works?

How does God use such occasions in our lives to test us, as He did with Philip?

What are His purposes in doing this?

How do Moses' words to Israel in the Old Testament book of Deuteronomy, chapter 8:1ff. relate to our experience as followers of Christ?

*OBJECTIONS FROM A FRIEND*

From the first chapter of the Gospel of John, it seems that Philip and Nathanael were good friends (John 1:44). Yet when Philip reports to Nathanael that "We have found the one Moses wrote about in the Law, and about whom the prophets also wrote—Jesus of Nazareth, the son of Joseph" ( John 1:45), he is met with skepticism from his friend Nathaniel. "Nazareth! Can any good come from there?"
How do you think this made Philip feel about his friend Nathanael?

Have you ever had a good friend display a similar negative attitude to you about spiritual issues?

If so, how did you handle it?

What are we to learn from the way Philip handled the situation with Nathanael?

What did he mean when he said to Nathanael, "Come and see" (John 1:46)?

What might we say to our friends who have similar objections?

# EXPRESSIONS

*"There is one church her, so I go to it. On Sunday mornings I quit the house and wander down the hill to the white frame church in the firs. On a big Sunday there might be twenty of us there; often I am the only person under sixty, and feel as though I'm on an archaeological tour of Soviet Russia. The man knows God. Once, in the middle of the long pastoral prayer of intercession for the whole world—for the gift of wisdom to its leaders, for hope and mercy to the grieving and pained, succor to the oppressed, and God's grace to all—in the middle of this he stopped, and burst out, 'Lord, we bring you these same petitions every week.' After a shocked pause, he continued reading the prayer. Because of this, I like him very much."*

--Annie Dillard, *Holy the Firm*

*"We ought perhaps to regard the miraculous, however rare, as the true Christian norm and ourselves as spiritual cripples."*

–C.S. Lewis, *Christian Reflections*

*"God instituted prayer to give man the dignity of causality."*

–Pascal, *Pensees*

# MEDITATIONS

*"And you shall remember all the way which the Lord your God had led you in the wilderness these forty years, that He might humble you, testing you, to know what was in your heart, whether you would keep His commandments or not. And He humbled you and let you be hungry, and fed you with manna which you did not know, nor did your fathers know, that He might make you understand that man does not live by bread alone, but man lives by everything that proceeds out of the mouth of the Lord."*

–Deuteronomy 8:2-3

*"And the Lord's bondservant must not be quarrelsome, but be kind to all, able to teach, patient when wronged, with gentleness correcting those who are in opposition, if perhaps God may grant them repentance leading to the knowledge of the truth…"*

–2 Timothy 2:24-25

# REFLECTIONS

MAY I ALWAYS BE GRATEFUL…that the God of the universe, in Jesus Christ, has sought me out and made His mercy known to me, and invited me to follow Him.

MAY I ALWAYS BE MINDFUL…that God may test our faith to see what is in our hearts.

MAY I ALWAYS BE HOPEFUL…that my friends who are not followers of Christ would consider His claims and love for them, and that they would "come and see."

**NOTES**

# Matthew

*A Man Like Me*

**The Story of a Man Who Took Forgiveness to Heart**

Matthew was arguably the most notorious of the disciples, and being a former tax collector was the last "credential" one would expect for one of the Twelve disciples of Christ! He was the brother of James the Less and both were the sons of Alphaeus. He is referred to by his Jewish name, "Levi, son of Alphaeus" in Mark 2:14 (see also Luke 5:27-29), and simply as "Matthew" in the lists of the Twelve disciples in Luke 6:15 and Acts 1:13. While we might expect to know a lot about Matthew, since he authored the Gospel that bears his name, the truth of the matter is that we know very little about him. He seems to have been content to stay in the background, since in his entire Gospel; he only mentions his own name twice (Matthew 9:9, 10:2-4).

It is hard for us today to fathom the hatred and disgust with which the Jewish people bore toward tax collectors employed by the Roman Empire. While there was legitimacy to some taxes being collected by the Romans as the ruling government (see Jesus' comments about rendering money to Caesar, Matthew 22:15-22, also Romans 13:6-7), oftentimes unscrupulous tax collectors would assess additional money for themselves. It is little wonder that the Talmud considered a man "righteous" if he lied or deceived a tax collector!

In Israel's day, there were two types of tax collectors, the *Gabbai* and the *Mokhes*. While the *Gabbai* were the general tax collectors, collecting taxes for property, income, and the poll tax, the *Mokhes* collected a duty on imports and exports, and goods for domestic trade. It was the *Mokhes* who often were most abusive and capricious in their collection of taxes. There was a further delineation among the *Mokhes* between the *Great Mokhes* and the *Little Mokhes*. The *Great Mokhes* were the "chief tax collectors," who hired other tax collectors to work for them (Zaccheus was apparently a chief tax-collector, see Luke 19:2), while the *Little Mokhes* were those who personally worked the tax collection booths. It seems that Matthew was considered to be a *Little Mokhes*, since he manned a tax office booth, working directly with people (see Matthew 9:9, Luke 5:27).

As Matthew had daily encounters with the Jewish people, collecting taxes from them, one can only imagine the derision and scorn he received from his own people. No self-respecting Jew would ever choose to be a tax collector! He surely would have been banned from worshipping at the synagogue, and bringing his sacrifice to the Temple. So when Jesus called Matthew to follow Him (Matthew 9:9), it had to come as a tremendous shock for a tax collector to receive such an invitation, and likewise those who witnessed this event had to be amazed that such a despised man would abandon his tax collection booth and follow Jesus.

Immediately after his decision to follow Jesus, the Scripture tells us that Matthew threw a great banquet for Jesus that evening, with Jesus' disciples as invitees, and with Jesus Himself as the guest of honor (Luke 5:29-30, Matthew 9:9-11). What is more, we are told that Matthew invited his fellow tax collectors and "many other notorious sinners" (Matthew 9:9) to the party, which raised the ire of the Pharisees who asked His disciples, "Why does your teacher eat with such scum?" (Matthew 9:11, Luke 5:30) Clearly, the riff-raff that Matthew had invited to the party honoring Jesus was not up to par with whom the Pharisees thought should have been attending this dinner party. "If he was a truly righteous rabbi," they reasoned, "he wouldn't be associating with such scum of society!" Yet Jesus' response is direct and unmistakable, "Healthy people don't need a doctor—sick people do. I have come to call sinners to turn from their sins, not to spend time with those who think they are already good enough" (Luke 5:31-32, Matthew 9:13 adds that Jesus said, "Now go and learn the meaning of this Scripture: 'I want you to be merciful; I don't want your sacrifices.'").

We may ask, what made a tax collector like Matthew make such a radical change in his life? Why would he "drop everything," so to speak, to follow this Jewish rabbi, Jesus? While both accounts of Matthew's call (Matthew 9 and Luke 5) might lead one to believe that Matthew haphazardly decided to leave his tax collection booth and follow Jesus, a careful reading of the preceding passages suggests that he had at least been privy to Jesus' teachings and miracles attesting to His Messiahship.

And although Matthew clearly had a good deal of wealth (Luke 5:29 says a "great" party was held for Jesus, His disciples, and his own friends – which suggests that he probably had a large home and the financial resources for such a celebration), there still seemed to be something missing in his life. Deep down, he knew that riches do not ultimately satisfy.

And not only did he recognize the futility of riches without God, he also seems to have been a Jew who was a true seeker, as he looked for the coming of the long-awaited Messiah. Being ostracized from the worshipping community in Israel because of his profession as a tax collector, there is every reason to believe that Matthew studied the Old Testament seriously on his own. His own Gospel shows a remarkable working knowledge of the Old Testament (he quotes from the Law, the Prophets, and the Psalms, each of the major sections of the Old Testament). And Matthew knew his "Bible" quite well, as he quotes in his own Gospel from the Old Testament some ninety-nine times, which is more than the Gospels of Mark, Luke, and John combined.

There is also something to be said, not only for the immediacy of his response to Jesus' invitation to be His disciple, but also because it was that *very* evening after deciding to follow Jesus, he threw a banquet for Jesus and His disciples, inviting the only people he knew – the dregs of this world. There was something genuine about Matthew's new found faith. It was a faith that, while it had no place for religious hypocrisy, welcomed the social outcasts of his world.

Interestingly, there are three tax collectors mentioned in the Gospels: the story of Zacchaeus, a chief tax collector (Luke 19:2-10); the parable of the publican and the Pharisee (Luke 18:10-14); and the story of Matthew's call to Jesus' invitation (Luke 5:27-28, Matthew 9:9). The central thread in all three of these stories is the idea of *forgiveness*, and that no matter how great a man's wealth or status in society; he deeply wants and needs to know that he can be forgiven whatever wrongs he has done. No doubt,

Matthew knew the greatness of his guilt in the dishonest extortion and oppression of his own people (see also Zacchaeus' comments in Luke 19:8, and the publican in Luke 18:13), but he also hungered for the promise of forgiveness, which Jesus offered. It was Jesus who said at that evening dinner party hosted by Matthew, "Healthy people don't need a doctor – sick people do. I have come to call sinners to turn from their sins, not to spend time with those who think they are already good enough." (Luke 5:31-32)

Tradition holds that Matthew, after the crucifixion and resurrection of Christ, ministered to the Jews both in Israel and abroad. Irenaeus, the church historian, suggests that he preached the Gospel among the Hebrews, which may include both those in Israel as well as Jews of the Dispersion. St. Ambrose links Matthew with Persia, which was on the primary trade route between Antioch and India. Furthermore, most traditions place Matthew in Ethiopia (either African or Asiatic, around the Caspian Sea near Persia), and that after many years of ministry, he was martyred for his faith by being burned at the stake, around A.D. 70.

Looking back over Matthew's life, it is hard to believe that Jesus would have chosen such a hated man to be one of His chosen disciples. Matthew himself needed no one to tell him he was a sinner. He was an exile, an outcast among his own people, and he knew the greatness of his guilt in extorting money from his own people. He understood that no matter how great a man's wealth, every man desperately wants to know that he can be forgiven. He was hoping for the Long-Awaited One who would come with healing in His hands to offer forgiveness, even at His command. In Jesus the Messiah, who had calmed the winds, stilled the sea, and invited him, "Follow Me," Matthew found it impossible to refuse the invitation. He could only marvel at such a mercy that could save a man like himself.

Matthew's life was not so different from our lives today. So many people today think they have done such horrible things, that God could *never* forgive them. Yet His offer is available to each one of us, who hunger for the promise of forgiveness. Jesus offers to come and take up residence within us by His Spirit, so we will never be alone. If we should hear His voice saying, "Come, Follow Me," can our hearts really refuse such an extravagant offer?

## DISCUSSION

*JUDGING OTHERS*

If you are part of a church or worshipping community, it is easy to have a tendency to look down on people like a Matthew, whose lives don't seem to "measure up" to ours. The Apostle Paul had the following advice for Christians who had a tendency to look down on people outside the church:

*"I have written you in my letter not to associate with immoral people—not at all meaning the people of this world who are immoral…In that case you would have to leave this world. But now I am writing you that you must not associate with anyone who calls himself a brother but is immoral…What business is it of mine to judge those outside the church? Are you not to judge those inside? God will judge those outside."*        -1 Corinthians 5:9-13

How do his words challenge us?

Do you have any "Matthews" in your life?

*WHO ARE OUR FRIENDS?*

Immediately following his decision to follow Jesus, Matthew held a great banquet for Jesus and His disciples, along with his fellow tax collectors and "other notorious sinners." It is often observed that when a person decides to follow Christ, they sever most of their social ties with their "B.C." (Before Christ) friends, and spend virtually all of their time with their new "Christian" friends. Do you think God wants you to sever your ties with your B.C. friends?

Why or why not?

Some have called the over emphasis on friendship among Christians, not *koivonia* (the Greek work for "fellowship"), but *koivonitis*, or "spiritual navel-gazing." Do you think this is a problem in the Christian community?

Are you and I guilty of "spiritual navel-gazing"?

If so, how can we go about changing this?

## SAFE VENUES

If we are followers of Jesus, while we will seek to lead holy lives, we will also try to maintain our relationships with those who are not followers of Christ. What are some ideas you can think of to create "safe venues" for those who are not followers of Christ to hear His message of forgiveness and redemption?

What activities or functions come to mind so that we could, following Jesus' example, become those who "have come to call sinners to turn from their sins, not to spend time with those who think they are already good enough"? (Luke 5:31-32)?

## GOOD ENOUGH FOR GOD

As a tax collector, Matthew surely was aware that he was a sinner. Yet he hungered for the forgiveness of his sins that only Jesus, the Promised Messiah, could offer. Many of us have a tendency to think that we need to have our "act together" before we decide to follow Christ. Do you ever wonder if you are *good enough* for God to accept you?

Why or why not?

Why do you think the non-religious people of Jesus' day were attracted to him, while the religious people were generally opposed to Him?

## THE GIFT OF ETERNAL LIFE

The apostle Paul states in Ephesians 2:8-9: "It is by grace that you have been saved, through faith, and this not from yourselves, it is the *gift* of God, not by works, so that no one can boast." How would you define "grace"?

If salvation is a gift, what are the implications of this?

What is the role of works or good deeds in one's life? How do Paul's words in the same passage cited above, verse 10, relate to works?

Check out Christ's words in Matthew 7:15-20, Paul's words in 2 Corinthians 13:5, and James words in James 2:14-26. What insight is provided from these verses to give us a biblical perspective about faith and works?

# EXPRESSIONS

*"When a man is getting better he understands more and more clearly the evil that is still left in him. When a man is getting worse, he understands his own badness less and less. A moderately bad man knows he is not very good: a thoroughly bad man thinks he is all right. This is common sense, really. You understand sleep when you are awake, not while you are sleeping. You can see mistakes in arithmetic when your mind is working properly: while you are making them you cannot see them. You can understand the nature of drunkenness when you are sober, not when you are drunk. Good people know about both good and evil: bad people do not know about either."*

–C. S. Lewis, *Mere Christianity*

*"One so often hears people say, 'I just can't handle it,' when they reject a biblical image of God as Father, as Lord or Judge; God as lover, as angry or jealous, God on a cross. I find this choice of words revealing, however real the pain they reflect: if we seek a God we can 'handle,' that will be exactly what we get. A God we can manipulate, suspiciously like ourselves, the wideness of whose mercy we've cut down to size."*

–Kathleen Norris, *Amazing Grace*

*"We are just itsy-bitsy people leading itsy-bitsy lives raising tomatoes when we could be raising Lazarus."*

–Novelist Annie Dillard

## MEDITATIONS

*"For it is by grace you have been saved, through faith, and this not from yourselves, it is the gift of God—not by works, so that no one can boast. For we are His workmanship, created in Christ Jesus to do go works, which God prepared in advance for us to do."*
–Ephesians 2:8-10

*"If God is for us, who can be against us? He who did not spare His own Son, but gave Him up for us all—how will he not also, along with Him, graciously give us all things! …Who shall separate us from the love of Christ? Shall trouble or hardship or persecution or famine or nakedness or danger or sword?…I am convinced that neither death nor life, neither angels nor demons, neither the present nor the future, nor any powers, neither height nor depth, nor anything else in all creation, will be able to separate us from the love of God that is in Christ Jesus our Lord."*
–Romans 8:31-39

## REFLECTIONS

MAY I ALWAYS BE GRATEFUL…that He has made my heart His home.

MAY I ALWAYS BE MINDFUL…of the greatness of God; great enough to calm the winds, still the seas, and call the universe into being, yet merciful enough to forgive a person like me.

MAY I ALWAYS BE HOPEFUL…that others may receive His forgiveness the same way that Matthew did.

# James the Great
## *Another Way*
### *Mercy Triumphs Over Judgment*

Although James is one of the three in Jesus' "inner circle," he is the least familiar to us. We know very little of him from the biblical accounts, and he is always paired with his younger, though more famous brother, John. Ironically, the only time James is singularly mentioned is when Luke tells of his martyrdom by King Herod (Acts 12:2), which is also the only martyrdom of a disciple mentioned in the New Testament.

While James might have been considered the logical choice to dominate the landscape among these inner circle disciples, it does not appear to have been the case. While he was the eldest son of Zebedee (the reason he always appears first when grouped with his brother), whose family seems to have been more prominent than the family of Peter and Andrew, we encounter complete silence about James. Nevertheless, his name comes immediately after Peter's in two of the lists of the apostles (Mark 3:16-19, Acts 1:13), suggesting that his influence was second only to Peter.

That James and John were sons of Zebedee, a prominent individual, is suggested by the reference to the sons simply as "the sons of Zebedee" (Matthew 20:20, 26:37, Mark 10:35, Luke 5:10, John 21:2). Zebedee's prestige came perhaps from his financial success as a fisherman, as well as his family lineage. His fishing business employed a number of hired servants (Mark 1:20), and the fact that James was known to the high priest, and able to get Peter admitted into the courtyard of the high priest the night Jesus was betrayed (John 18:15-16), suggests that Zebedee may have been a Levite, and even closely related to the high priest's family.

While James was not as prominent as his brother John or the disciple Peter, he nevertheless was part of the inner circle of three. He, Peter, and John were the only disciples that Jesus permitted to be with Him when He raised Jairus' daughter from the dead (Mark 5:37), witness His own glory on the Mount of Transfiguration (Matthew 17:1), and to be included with Jesus as He prayed in the Garden of Gethsemane (Mark 14:33).

What we do know of James is that he was a man of great *passion*. Nicknamed by Jesus, *Boanerges*, "Sons of Thunder" (Mark 3:17, the only reference in Scripture), both he and John had fiery temperaments. This zealous, passionate disposition is perhaps best seen in Luke 9:51-56, as Jesus is preparing to pass through Samaria on His way to Jerusalem. When the messengers of Jesus are refused by the Samaritans as they attempt to make plans for Jesus' arrival, both James and John, hearing of their rejection, asks Jesus: "Lord, should we order down fire from heaven to burn them up? But Jesus turned and rebuked them. So they went on to another village" (Luke 9:54-56). These "Sons of Thunder" were filled with zealous outrage, and were alluding to an Old Testament episode when the prophet Elijah confronted the pagan worship of Ahaziah, the son and successor of Ahab, and his wife, Jezebel.

Let's revisit this amazing story. When Ahaziah had fallen through the lattice of his upper chamber, and was seriously injured, he sent messengers to Baal-Zebub, the god of Ekron, to see whether he would recover from the injury (2 Kings 1). This false god, Baal-Zebub (which meant literally "god of dung"), represented the epitome of false worship. For a king of Israel to consult a pagan deity about his future represented the height of apostasy (see further Luke 11:15, which suggests that by the time of Christ, the name BEELZEBUB had become a way to refer to Satan). So when Elijah encountered these messengers, and they returned to Ahaziah to describe the prophet who met them, the king knew clearly that it was Elijah the Tishbite.

Subsequently, Ahaziah decided to have Elijah killed, and sent a captain with fifty men to arrest him and bring him back for his execution. When the captain spoke to Elijah, saying, "Man of God, the king has said, 'Come down!'" (2 Kings 9:9). Elijah, unfazed by the regiment that had arrived to arrest him, calmly replied, "If I am a man of God, then let fire come down from heaven and consume you and your fifty men.' And fire came down from heaven and consumed him and his fifty" (verse 10). Ahaziah was a foolish and arrogant king, so he repeated his command, sending fifty more soldiers to arrest Elijah – all with the same result! Again, a third time he commanded a captain to take fifty men to arrest him, but this time, the captain approached Elijah in humility and pleaded for the lives of him and his men, and Elijah went with them personally to deliver his prophecy to Ahaziah.

So when these fiery brothers, James and John, asked permission of Jesus to call down fire from heaven to consume this Samaritan village, they were clearly alluding to the story of Elijah in 2 Kings 1. What's more, this entire episode of Elijah's triumph over King Ahaziah had taken place in this same region of Samaria where the disciples wanted to bring down judgment upon this inhospitable village.

While the Sons of Thunder were confident they were on solid ground when they made their petition to Jesus, it was a different time, and their response to the Samaritan "slight" did not fit the mission of Jesus, who had a much different mission than that of Elijah: "He turned and rebuked them, and said, 'You do not know what manner of spirit you are of. For the Son of Man did not come to destroy men's lives but to save them'" (Luke 9:55-56). Furthermore, their request had a tinge of pride and arrogance, as they brazenly asked the Lord: "Do You want *us* to command fire to come down from heaven and consume them?"

All of the disciples, led by these Sons of Thunder, had a righteous indignation against this Samaritan village that had refused the Messiah hospitality. But soon they would come to understand that He was on a mission to rescue, not judge, people: "The Son of Man has come to seek and to save that which was lost" (Luke 19:10). A few years after this incident, after Christ's crucifixion and resurrection, as the early church began to grow beyond the borders of Jerusalem and Judea, Philip "went down to the city of Samaria and preached Christ to them" (Acts 8:5). There is every reason to believe that a number who were saved under Philip's ministry were some of the very same people whom Jesus had spared when James and John had wanted to bring fire down in judgment.

In addition to the episode in Luke 9, we see another "dark" side to the sons of Zebedee when they ask of Jesus a favor. In Mark 10, we are told that James and John made a request of Jesus, that in His glorious kingdom, they each would "sit in places of honor next to You, one at Your right hand and the other at Your left." In Matthew 20, the story is slightly different (which is *not* a contradiction, only supplementation), as James and John appear to have enlisted their mother to make this request of Jesus, that her sons have the two preeminent places of honor when His kingdom comes.

What makes this detail of the account in Matthew 20 so interesting is that when we examine Matthew 27:56 and Mark 16:1, we discover that the mother of James and John was named Salome. She was "one of the many women who followed Jesus from Galilee, ministering to Him" (Matthew 27:55). Because the Zebedee family was prominent and affluent, she may have joined here sons for extensive periods of time, traveling with the company of Jesus and His disciples. Some have also suggested that Salome was the sister of Mary, the mother of Jesus, and if this was the case, then her request would surely have carried a certain power, and would have been somewhat understandable (Matthew 28:55, Mark 15:40, Luke 23:49, John 19:25).

But as we know from the rest of the Scriptures leading up to Christ's death, these two brothers' ambitions ultimately created conflicts among the rest of the disciples, because the question of who deserved, or would get, the seats of honor became the supreme debate among them all—and was carried right up to the night of Jesus' betrayal (Luke 22:24).

Yet, as Jesus would reveal to them, while these Sons of Zebedee wanted the cup of glory, they, and James in particular, would be given the cup of suffering. They wanted power, but Jesus took up the towel and redefined greatness in terms of servanthood. Fourteen years after the upper room experience with Jesus, James would become the first of the disciples to be slain for his faith, in approximately A.D. 47. As mentioned earlier, James' martyrdom is the only apostle whose death is actually recorded in Scripture. Luke tells us in Acts 12:1-3: "Now about that time Herod the king stretched out his hand to harass some from the church. Then he killed James the brother of John with the sword. And because he saw that it pleased the Jews, he proceeded further to seize Peter also."

Eusebius, a trusted historian of the early church, has passed on an account of James' death that he received from Clement of Alexandria: "Clement says that the one who led James to the judgment seat, when he saw him bearing his testimony, was moved, and confessed that he was himself also a Christian. They were both, he says, led away together; and on the way he begged James to forgive him. And James, after considering a little, said, 'Peace be with Thee,' and kissed him. And thus they were both beheaded at the same time" (Eusebius, *Ecclesiastical Church History*, 2.9.2-3).

It has been observed that early on in their ministries, while the disciple Andrew, Peter's brother, drew men to Christ; James was content to bring judgment upon them. James and John had been confident that Jesus would grant their wish to call down fire from heaven upon that Samaritan village. Yet in the end, they would learn the "better way" of Andrew, of bringing men to the Savior rather than judging them, for "mercy triumphs over judgment" (James 2:13). While they had been consumed with extracting justice, making the guilty pay, Christ showed them Another Way.

Most of us are like James. We would prefer to see people judged, bowed before the judgment of the Living Word. Left up to us, no grace would be given. Yet the Scriptures tell us, "*all* have sinned and fall short of the glory of God" (Romans 3:23). When we examine our own hearts, we, like James, can rejoice that the grace of God now overflows in Jesus Christ. It is only mercy that brings the barrier down between God and ourselves—only mercy speaks to our human hearts.

# DISCUSSION

## PASSIONATE PEOPLE

James the Great and his brother the apostle John were nicknamed by Jesus, "Sons of Thunder" (Mark 3:17).  What do you think of Christians who have a fiery, passionate personality?

Would you say this is generally a good thing? Why or why not?

## TAKING REVENGE

What do you think of James and John asking Jesus if they could call down fire from heaven on the Samaritan village that refused hospitality to Jesus and His disciples (Luke 9:51ff.)?

Do you believe they thought Jesus would approve of what they wanted to do? Why or why not?

Was the indignation they felt toward this Samaritan village a righteous indignation?

## RELIGIOUS POWER PLAYS

As part of Jesus' inner circle of disciples, it appears that their close relationship with Jesus led them to request places of honor when He came in His kingdom. Were they wrong to make such a request of Jesus?

Why or why not?

Have you ever seen religious "power plays" in ministries?

If so, what do you think is the root of these abuses?

Many of us are a lot like James the Great. We would prefer God to judge people for their sins instead of extending mercy to them. Why do you think we feel this way?

James, the author of the epistle of James (a different James, the half brother of our Lord) says "mercy triumphs over judgment" (James 2:13). What do you think he meant by this phrase?

How do Paul's words in Romans 3:23, that "all have sinned and fall short of the glory of God," help us to properly view ourselves and others, along with their shortcomings?

Is there someone in your life that you need to extend mercy and forgiveness to?

# EXPRESSIONS

*"There is a poem by the literary critic C. S. Lewis that is more or less a confession. The first time I read it I identified so strongly with his sentiments, I felt as though somebody were calling my name. I always come back to this poem when I think soberly about my faith, about the general precepts that indicate we are flawed, all of us are flawed, the corrupt politician and the pious Sunday school teacher. In the poem C. S. Lewis faces himself. He addresses his own depravity with a soulful sort of bravery: 'All this is flashy rhetoric about loving you, I never had a selfless thought since I was born. I am mercenary and self-seeking through and through; I want God, you, all friends, merely to serve my turn…Peace, reassurance, pleasure, are the goals I seek, I cannot crawl one inch outside my proper skin; I talk of love—a scholar's parrot may talk Greek—But, self-imprisoned, always end where I begin.' I sat there above the city wondering if I was like the parrot in Lewis's poem, swinging in my cage, reciting Homer, all the while having no idea what I was saying…"*

–Donald Miller, *Blue Like Jazz: Nonreligious Thoughts on Christian Spirituality*

*"When we get our spiritual house in order, we'll be dead. This goes on. You arrive at enough certainty to be able to make your way, but it is making it in darkness. Don't expect faith to clear things up for you. It is trust, not certainty."*

—Flannery O'Connor

*"I believe there is one (Christian virtue) even more unpopular. It is laid down in the Christian rule, 'Thou shalt love thy neighbor as thyself.' Because in Christian morals 'thy neighbor' includes 'thy enemy', and so we come up against this terrible duty of forgiving our enemies. Everyone says forgiveness is a lovely idea, until they have something to forgive…Loving my enemies does not apparently mean thinking them nice either. That is an enormous relief. For a good many people imagine that forgiving your enemies means making out that they are really not much bad fellows after all, when it is quite plain that they are. Go a step further. In most clear-sighted moments not only do I not think myself a nice man, but I know that I am a very nasty one…I remember Christian teachers telling me long ago that I must hate a bad man's actions, but not hate the bad man: or, as they would say, hate the sin but not the sinner."*

—C. S. Lewis, *Mere Christianity*

## MEDITATIONS

*"Do not judge, lest you be judged yourselves. For in the way you judge, you will be judged; and by your standard of measure, it shall be measured to you. And why do you look at the speck in your brother's eye, but do not notice the log that is in your own eye? Or how can you say to your brother, 'Let me take the speck out of your eye,' and behold, the log is in your own eye? You hypocrite, first take the log out of your own eye, and then you will see clearly enough to take the speck out of your brother's eye."*

–Matthew 7:1-5

*"For just as you once were disobedient to God but now have been shown mercy because of their disobedience, so these also now have been disobedient, in order that because of the mercy shown to you they also may now be shown mercy. For God has shot up all in disobedience that He might show mercy to all. Oh, the depth of the riches both of the wisdom and knowledge of God! How unsearchable are His judgments and unfathomable His ways!"*

–Romans 11:30-33

## REFLECTIONS

MAY I ALWAYS BE GRATEFUL…that God has not judged me according to my sins, but has extended His mercy to me in Jesus Christ.

MAY I ALWAYS BE MINDFUL…that those of us who are followers of Christ are often prone to judging others, and religious power plays, and that I will be judged in the same way that I have judged others.

MAY I ALWAYS BE HOPEFUL…that those who do not know Christ may open their hearts and minds to the forgiveness available to them from God.

# Nathanael
*Only God Would Know*
### God Sees the Heart

Nathanael is always listed in the four lists of the apostles as Bartholomew, while in John he is always referred to as *Nathanael*. While Bartholomew is a Hebrew surname meaning, "son of Tolmai," the name Nathanael means, "God has given."

In the Synoptic Gospels (Matthew, Mark, and Luke) and the Book of Acts, we have no details of Nathanael, and they in fact only mention him once, when they list all twelve of the disciples. It is only in John's Gospel, and only in two passages, that we really know anything of Nathanael. We are told in John 21:2 that Nathanael's hometown was Cana in Galilee, which was very close to Jesus' hometown of Nazareth, and also the place where Jesus performed His first miracle, turning the water into wine at a wedding (John 2:11).

There is strong Biblical evidence that Nathanael, along with Philip, Thomas, James and John (the sons of Zebedee), and Peter and Andrew, were all fishermen from Galilee, and were probably companions long before Jesus called them to be His disciples. After the resurrection, when the apostles returned to Galilee, Peter remarked, "I am going fishing" (John 21:3), and the others with him all answered, "We are going with you also." According to John 21:2, that group included Peter, Thomas, Nathanael, the sons of Zebedee, and "two others," who were most likely Philip and Andrew, as they are frequently seen to be in the company of this group of fishermen.

Most of what we know of Nathanael comes from the first chapter of John's Gospel, which details his call to discipleship. Nathanael's invitation to follow Jesus came on the heels of Jesus' baptism, when John the Baptist declared that Jesus is the Christ, the Lamb of God who takes away the sins of the world (John 1:29). Whereas Andrew, John, and Peter (and possibly James) were the first disciples to be called while Jesus was in the wilderness, it was on the following day, as Jesus planned on going to Galilee, that Jesus sought out Philip, who was from Bethsaida, the same hometown as Andrew and Peter (John 1:44). Because Nathanael was brought to Jesus by Philip immediately after his own call to discipleship, many have rightly suggested that Philip and Nathanael were close friends. Similarly, in the Gospel accounts, like the brothers Peter and Andrew, and James and John, Philip and Nathanael, though not actual brothers, appear to be close companions.

According to John 1:45, immediately after Philip's call by Jesus, he went out to find Nathanael, telling him: "We have found Him of whom Moses in the law, and also the prophets, wrote. His name is Jesus, the son of Joseph from Nazareth." The fact that Philip introduced Jesus this way suggests that Nathanael had a reverence and respect for the Old Testament, and knew well the Messianic prophecies about the Christ. There is good reason to believe that both Philip and Nathanael had studied the Old Testament together, and were probably together in the wilderness to hear John the Baptist immediately before Jesus' invitation (John 1:35ff.).

What the reader of John's Gospel cannot be prepared for is Nathanael's brazen response to Philip's excitement about possibly finding the Christ: "Nazareth. Can any good thing come out of Nazareth?" (John 1:46) While Nathanael could have at least attempted to raise an objection to Jesus, since He was from the small town of Nazareth, his response reveals his disdain for Nazareth. While Jews in Jesus' day who resided in Judea had an abhorrence for all Galileans (north of Jerusalem), even *other* Galileans looked down upon the people from Nazareth. So Nathanael, though he was from the small, insignificant town of Cana, was simply echoing the common contempt all Galileans had for the town of Nazareth. That Jesus was from the despised, inconsequential town of Nazareth reminds us that God often delights to use the common, profane, weak, and lowly things of this world to confound that which is considered powerful by the world's standards (cf. 1 Corinthians 1:27).

Although Nathanael revealed his contempt for the town of Nazareth, his own hometown of Cana was not exactly considered a prestigious town, either. While Cana was a side trip from everything, Nazareth was at least a crossroads for people traveling from the Mediterranean to the land of Galilee. Similarly, one of the main travel routes between Jerusalem and Lebanon (going north and south) passed through Nazareth. So Nathanael's criticism of Nazareth as being a "backwoods" town doesn't fully explain his prejudice. Rivalry and civic pride between the two towns may help explain his negative response to Philip's excitement.

Prejudice blinded Nathanael from initially believing that the Messiah could come from such an uncultured, contemptible community as Nazareth. And on a greater scale, the prejudice of the nation and its religious leaders blinded them from recognizing Jesus as the Messiah. To these cultural sophisticates of the Jewish nation, it was inconceivable that the Messiah and his apostles would come from the "backwoods" of Galilee (cf. John 7:52). Likewise, this also happened in Jesus' own town, in His own synagogue, where He had grown up. The people in Nazareth were filled with such hatred and disdain that they tried to take Him to a cliff on the edge of town and throw Him off to kill Him (Luke 4:22ff.).

Yet, fortunately for Nathanael, his prejudice didn't ultimately keep him from considering Christ. His friend Philip had said to him, "Come and see" (John 1:46), and Nathanael did just that. When he first approached Jesus, the first words he heard the Messiah utter were, "Behold, an Israelite *indeed* in whom is no deceit!" (John 1:47). Because Jesus was God, and knew all men's hearts (John 2:25), Jesus knew Nathanael already. Whatever we may think of Nathanael's prejudices, Jesus knew his character, that he was pure-hearted. While his prejudice is seen in his initial response to Philip's excitement about their finding the Messiah, Nathanael was no hypocrite. His love for God and his search for the Messiah, were sincere.

Jesus proclaims that Nathanael was an "Israelite *indeed*." The root meaning of this Greek word, *alethos*, means that which is "authentic, genuine." This commendation of Nathanael was not a reference to his ancestry (being a descendent of Abraham), but rather his heart-condition, his guilelessness. While much of the nation of Israel were hypocrites, wearing a façade of spirituality (Matthew 23:13-33), Nathanael was the real thing.

And because his heart was pure, we see his true character revealed in his response to Jesus' amazing statement about his own character: "Nathanael said to Him, 'How do you know me?'" (John 1:48) It is hard to determine exactly what Nathanael was saying by his response. True, his friend Philip had brought him to Jesus, but at this point in time he still had to be wondering, questioning whether this Jesus could possibly be the long-awaited Messiah. So by his question, "How do you know me?" he may have been saying, "Are you flattering me? Are you trying to make me one of your followers by complimenting me? How could you possibly know me?"

Jesus' answer to Nathanael's inquiry was meant to convey to Nathanael that He is no mere prophet: "Before Philip called you, when you were under the fig tree, *I saw you*" (John 1:48). Immediately, Nathanael realized that he was dealing with Someone who could even see into his heart, and know his motivations and inclinations, an ability that resides only with God (cf. Psalm 139:1ff.). Some scholars have suggested that there may be significance in Jesus' allusion to the fig tree, since this was often a place of meditation and reflection among the Israelites. In essence, Jesus was declaring to Nathanael, "Not only did I see you under the fig, but I also know what you were doing – you were meditating, reading, and praying, reflecting on the Scriptures that speak of Me."

This, essentially, was the convincing proof for Nathanael: "Rabbi, you are the Son of God! You are the King of Israel!" (John 1:49) Clearly, Nathanael's comprehension of the Old Testament prophecies concerning the Messiah, the King of Israel, were finding their fulfillment in his encounter with Jesus (cf. Psalm 2, Zephaniah 3:15, Micah 5:2). And as John tells us at the end of his Gospel, that he wrote it to demonstrate that Jesus is the Son of God (John 20:31), so here, early on in his Gospel, we see a bold presentation through Nathanael's encounter with Jesus that this One is the Messiah, the Son of God.

Jesus' next statement to Nathanael was intended to further demonstrate that He was the fulfillment of the Old Testament Scriptures: "Jesus answered and said to him, 'Because I said to you, "I saw you under the fig tree," do you believe? You will see greater things than these.' And He said to him, 'Most assuredly, I say to you, hereafter you shall see heaven open, and the angels of God ascending and descending upon the Son of Man'" (John 1:51). Jesus here not only affirmed Nathanael's new-found faith, but also assured him that in the future he would witness even greater things to convince him that Jesus was the Son of God and the King of Israel.

Interestingly, Jesus' allusion in John 1:51 to the "angels of God ascending and descending upon the Son of Man," finds its background in the Old Testament, where the patriarch Jacob had a dream. In this dream, Jacob saw a "ladder that was set up on earth, and its top reached to heaven; and there the angels of God were ascending and descending on it" (Genesis 28:12). As the vision Jacob had of the ladder that stretched into the heavens was a visual confirmation of God's presence with him in the Promised Land of Israel, so Jesus is here declaring that *He* is the Ladder *par excellence* that connects heaven and earth. *He* is the Bridge of communication between His Heavenly Father and the world He came to redeem.

Aside from this passage from the first chapter of John's Gospel, this is all we know of Nathanael from the Scriptures. Some church traditions suggest that his missionary endeavors led him to Persia and India, and even as far as Armenia. The manner of his death, said to have occurred at Albanopolis in Armenia, is equally uncertain. According to some, he was beheaded, according to others, flayed alive and crucified, head downward, by order of Astriagis, for having converted his brother, Polymius, the King of Armenia, in approximately A.D. 62. On account of this latter legend, he is often represented in art (e.g. Michelangelo's masterpiece, *The Last Judgment*) as bald, massive, grizzled, as he gazes towards his Master as if angrily awaiting the judgment of his enemies. In his right hand the apostle holds aloft the knife with which he was skinned, and in his left his empty, rumpled skin, the token of his martyrdom.

Yet looking back over Nathanael's life of dedication to Christ, his giving up his own life for Christ, he would have thought a small price. His many years of searching, watching, and praying for the promised Messiah—the Prophet, Priest, and King—had finally come true. In Jesus, whose eyes had seen right through him, and into his soul, he realized that he had encountered the One who completely knew him. And what was true for Nathanael is also true for each of us, that the omniscient Lord of Everything knows us intimately, even before a word is on our tongue, "Thou dost know it all" (Psalm 139:1-3), as only God would know.

# DISCUSSION

## WHAT GOOD CAN COME FROM NAZARETH?

It seems from John's Gospel that Philip and Nathanael were good friends. When Philip tells him, "We have found Him who Moses in the Law wrote about…His name is Jesus, the son of Joseph from Nazareth" (John 1:45), Nathanael responds, "Nazareth? What good can come from there?" (John 1:46) Why do you think Nathanael responded so negatively?

## SMALL TOWN RIVALRY

Nathanael's response may suggest he had some prejudice or contempt toward Nazareth, Jesus' hometown.  What are some examples of prejudice that you have observed by people of faith?

How do the New Testament passages of James 2:1-13 and 1 Corinthians 1:27 address this issue of prejudice?

What are some of the greatest challenges you face as you attempt to treat all people fairly?

## KNOWN BY GOD

When Nathanael first met Jesus, the first words said to him by Jesus were: "Behold, an Israelite *indeed* in whom is no deceit!" (John 1:47) When Nathanael questioned Jesus, "How do you know me?" Jesus tells him, "Before Philip called you, when you were under the fig tree, I saw you" (John 1:48).  What point do you think Jesus was making to Nathanael by telling him this?

What was Nathanael possibly doing under the fig tree when Jesus saw him?

How might David's words of Psalm 139:1ff. apply to Nathanael's encounter with Jesus?

What does this suggest about the identity of Jesus?

Read through Psalm 139. What thoughts come to mind about the Living God, who knows all our thoughts and words, even before we ever utter a word?

How does this knowledge that God has affect the psalmist?

How does this knowledge that God has affect you and me?

*JACOB'S LADDER*

After Nathanael declares that Jesus is the Son of God, the King of Israel (John 1:49), Jesus tells him, "You will see greater things than that…I tell you the truth, you shall see heaven open, and the angels of God *ascending and descending* on the Son of Man" (John 1:51). What could Jesus have been referring to?

How does the story of "Jacob's Ladder," the story of Jacob's dream as he is leaving the Promised Land (Genesis 28), possibly shed light on Jesus' words to Nathanael?

How might Jesus be using this story to refer to Himself?

# EXPRESSIONS

*"I sometimes pray not for self-knowledge in general but for just so much self-knowledge at the moment as I can bear and use at the moment; the little daily dose. Have we any reason to suppose that total self-knowledge, if it were given us, would be for our good? Children and fools, we are told, should never look at half-done work; and we are not yet, I trust, even half-done."*

-C. S. Lewis, *Letters to Malcolm: Chiefly on Prayer*

*"We crave nothing less than perfect story; and while we chatter or listen all our lives in a din of craving— jokes, anecdotes, novels, dreams, films, plays, songs, half the words of our days—we are satisfied only by the one short tale we feel to be true: History is the will of a just god who knows us."*

–Reynolds Price, *A Palpable God*

*"So now, from this mad passion*
*Which made me take art for an idol and a king*
*I have learnt the burden of error that it bore*
*And what misfortune springs from man's desire…*
*The world's frivolities have robbed me of the time*
*That I was given for reflecting upon God."*

-Michelangelo

## MEDITATIONS

*"Brothers, think of what you were when you were called. Not many of you were wise by human standards; not many were influential; not many were of noble birth. But God chose the foolish things of the world to shame the wise; God chose the weak things of the world to shame the strong. He chose the lowly things of this world and the despised things—and the things that are not—to nullify the things that are, so that no one may boast before him. It is because of him that you are in Christ Jesus, who has become for us wisdom from God—that is, our righteousness, holiness, and redemption. Therefore, as it is written: 'Let him who boasts boast in the Lord'."*

–1 Corinthians 1:26-31

*"O Lord, you have searched me and you know me. You know when I sit and when I rise; you perceive my thoughts from afar. You discern my going out and my lying down; you are familiar with all my ways. Before a word is on my tongue you know it completely, O Lord. You hem me in—behind and before; you have laid your hand upon me. Such knowledge is too wonderful for me, too lofty for me to attain…"*

–Psalm 139:1-6

## REFLECTIONS

MAY I ALWAYS BE GRATEFUL…that God's mercy is extended not just to the powerful, the high and mighty, but to all who's heart sincerely seek Him.

MAY I ALWAYS BE MINDFUL…that God not only knows my actions, but also my heart.

MAY I ALWAYS BE HOPEFUL…that those who seek Him would put away their prejudices and skepticism when considering Christ and His invitation to follow Him.

**NOTES**

# James the Less
## *Even the Least*
### **No Ordinary People**

We encounter various men named "James" in the pages of the New Testament. There is James, one of the sons of Zebedee, whose brother was the beloved disciple John. This James was known as "James the Great," and would become the first martyr among the disciples (Acts 12:1-3). There is also another James, generally referred to as "James the Righteous," who was the son of Mary and Joseph, and therefore a half-brother of Christ (Galatians 1:19). James the Righteous would become a leader of the church in Jerusalem, as seen by his important role played at the Jerusalem Council (Acts 15:13-21). He is likewise thought to be the same James who penned the New Testament epistle that bears his name, one of the earliest books of the New Testament.

But the James with whom we are concerned is referred to as "the son of Alphaeus" (Matthew 10:3, Mark 3:18, Luke 6:15, Acts 1:13). He is also generally considered to be the brother of the apostle Levi Matthew, also referred to as a "son of Alphaeus" (Mark 2:14). Their mother was Mary (Mark 15:40), and when we compare Mark 15:40 with Matthew 27:56 and Mark 15:47, it is generally understood that she had another son named Joses, who was a well-known follower of Christ, yet who was not an apostle. This mother of these sons, Mary, was clearly a devoted follower of Christ, as she appears with Mary Magdalene and Mary the mother of the sons of Zebedee as eyewitnesses of Christ's crucifixion, as well as coming with the women to prepare Christ's body for burial (Mark 15:47, Matthew 27:56, Mark 16:1).

An interesting reference to this James, the son of Alphaeus, is that in Mark 15:40, he is referred to as, "James the *Less*." The Greek word for "Less" is *micros*, and its primary meaning is "small in stature," so probably refers to his physical frame, but could refer to his age. This latter meaning, of being youthful, could very well be the significance of the title, as it would distinguish him from James the Great, the son of Zebedee, the disciple John's brother.

Clearly, James the Less was not as influential as James the Great or James the Righteous. While James the Great had come from the prominent Zebedee family (well known by the high priest, John 18:15-16), and James the Righteous was the half-brother of Jesus, James the Less had no particular claim to fame. It may very well be that James the Less was a man of quiet demeanor, who remained in the background, with no strong leadership skills like some of the other disciples. And yet, while only his name remains, he was *still* one of the Twelve that were chosen by the Lord, trained and equipped by Him, for the single purpose of going out and bearing witness with the other disciples. Early church history likewise is virtually silent about him. And while some of the early traditions confuse him with James the Righteous, the Lord's half-brother, there is some evidence that James the Less carried the Gospel to Syria and Persia. Accounts of his martyrdom also differ widely. While some traditions say he was stoned to death, others say he was crucified, or beaten to death, perhaps in Jerusalem around A.D. 63.

Despite being a virtual "No-Name," James the Less, who lived out his days in virtual obscurity, still bore witness to the saving power of personally knowing Jesus Christ. Having been with the Messiah, like the other disciples, he too was empowered to go out and change the world. James the Less reminds us that while most of us will not achieve fame or fortune in this life, even the least of us can have a significant impact in our world. As we seek to play out our parts faithfully in the human drama, we should be mindful that it is only when the final curtain falls, that we will know our place in eternity. Even the least of us, who are called to His table of fellowship, can change the world through living by the power of His love.

# DISCUSSION

*ALL PEOPLE MATTER*

Although James the Less is listed as one of the Twelve, we know so little about him. What does this say about the individual, irrespective of his or her fame or recognition in this life?

G. K. Chesterton once observed, "All men matter. You matter. I matter. It's the hardest thing in theology to believe." What do you think that he was saying by this statement?

*CELEBRITY WORSHIP*

In his book, *The Image*, Daniel Boorstin made the following observation: "One of the oldest of man's visions was the flash of divinity in the great man…Two centuries ago when a great man appeared, people looked for God's purpose in him; today we look for his press agent." What point do you think he was making?

In our culture, where the worship of celebrity is commonplace (athletes, movie stars, high profile Christians, etc.), what do you think we should learn from the life of James the Less?

*LIFE A SACRED DRAMA*

Malcolm Muggeridge once observed that all of life is a "sacred" drama. What do you think he meant by this phrase?

How does such a view of life differ so dramatically from the way most of us think about our lives?

If life is in fact a "sacred drama," a spiritual journey, what are the implications of this for our lives?

*THE GREATEST TRUTH IN THE WORLD*

The famous German theologian Karl Barth was once asked, "Dr. Barth, in all your theological studies throughout your life, what have you come to believe is the greatest theological truth that you've ever learned?" Barth answered without hesitation, "Jesus loves me this I know, for the Bible tells me so..." What do you think of Barth's response?

What's the significance of this statement to your life?

*THE ORDINARY LIFE*

Despite being a virtual "No-Name", James the Less, who lived out his days in virtual obscurity, still bore witness to the saving power of personally knowing Jesus Christ, and was empowered to go out, like the other disciples, and make a difference in the world. Tradition suggests that he may have carried the Gospel to Syria and Persia, and was possibly martyred in Jerusalem around A.D. 63. He is a healthy reminder that while most of us will not achieve fame or fortune in this present life, even the least of us can have a significant impact in our spheres of influence. Can you think of someone who would be considered one of the least that has accomplished much or touched many lives in spite of their limitations?

Where has God placed you to play your part in the sacred drama of life?

Are we mindful that only when the final curtain falls, we will then know how much of a difference we made in the world?

What are the obstacles that keep us from having this kind of eternal perspective?

# EXPRESSIONS

*"Do not forget that the value and interest of life is not so much to do conspicuous things…as to do ordinary things with the perception of their enormous value."*

–Pierre Teilhard de Chardin

*"Inspection stickers used to have printed on the back 'Drive carefully—the life you save may be your own.' That is the wisdom of men in a nutshell. What God says, on the other hand, is 'The life you save is the life you lose.' In other words, the life you clutch, hoard, guard, and play safe with is in the end a life worth little to anybody, including yourself; and only a life given away for love's sake is a life worth living. To bring His point home, God shows us a man who gave His life away to the extent of dying a national disgrace without a penny in the bank or a friend to His name. In terms of men's wisdom, he was a perfect fool, and anybody who thinks he can follow Him without making something like the same kind of fool of himself is laboring under not a cross but a delusion."*

–Frederick Buechner, "Wishful Thinking"

*"It may be possible for each to think too much of his own potential glory hereafter; it is hardly possible for him to think to often or too deeply about that of his neighbor…There are no ordinary people. You have never talked to a mere mortal. Nations, cultures, arts, civilization—these are mortal, and their life is to ours as the life of a gnat. But it is immortals whom we joke with, work with, marry, snub, and exploit—immortal horrors or everlasting splendors."*

–C. S. Lewis, "The Weight of Glory"

## MEDITATIONS

*"For you created my inmost being; you knit me together in my mother's womb. I praise you because I am fearfully and wonderfully made; your works are wonderful, I know that full well. My frame was not hidden from you when I was made in the secret place. When I was woven together in the depths of the earth, your eyes saw my unformed body. All the days ordained for me were written in your book before one of them came to be."*

–Psalm 139: 13-16

*"I pray also that the eyes of your heart may be enlightened in order that you may know the hope to which He has called you, the riches of his glorious inheritance in the saints, and His incomparably great power for us who believe. That power is like the working of His mighty strength, which He exerted in Christ when He raised Him from the dead and seated Him at His right hand in the heavenly realms, far above all rule and authority, power and dominion, and every title that can be given, not only in the present age but also in the one to come."*

–Ephesians 1:18-21

## REFLECTIONS

MAY I ALWAYS BE GRATEFUL…that my true worth will not be determined by fame and fortune, but how I used what was entrusted to me.

MAY I ALWAYS BE MINDFUL…that even though many of us lead simple lives in obscurity, with no acclaim and are seldom recognized, there are no "ordinary" people. Even the least can change the world if they will do their part.

MAY I ALWAYS BE HOPEFUL…that those who work in silence behind the scenes will live in the power of God's love, just as James the Less did.

# Thomas
## *Where I Was*
### *He Met Me Where I Was*

*Doubting Thomas.* His very name has become a byword of derision through the centuries when this follower of Jesus is mentioned alongside the other apostles. Truth be known, this is about all most people know of Thomas. We imagine him as a pessimistic, dour follower of Jesus, disinclined to believe, despite the overwhelming evidence. Here, conventional wisdom reasons, was the man who tried to throw a monkey wrench into the engine of Easter Joy! But this is not the whole story, or even an accurate portrayal of the man who, tradition tells us, would faithfully carry the Gospel to the Orient. Ancient traditions suggest that Thomas carried the Gospel as far as India, where he would be buried, near the city of Madras.  And there are churches in the south of India that tradition suggests were founded under his ministry. Let's see if we can paint a more accurate picture of the real Thomas.

Actually, the information about Thomas in the New Testament does not lead the reader to such a negative, foregone conclusion. Like most of the other disciples, Thomas is mentioned only a few times, but those vignettes present him as a courageous man, known for his intellect and clear thinking. Interestingly, we know more about the life of Thomas *after* Calvary than we do about any of the other apostles with the exception of Peter and John. Furthermore, almost the entire extent of his ministry took place outside the Roman Empire, and most of our sources about him are non-Western. If he is the poster-boy of failure among the disciples, how do we account for this change of heart?

While Thomas is mentioned only once by each of the Gospel writers Matthew, Mark, and Luke, it is the apostle John who gives us a "zoom lens" snapshot of this complex follower of Jesus. While John mentions Thomas, who was also called "Didymus" (meaning the Twin, John 11:16) four times in his Gospel, the last occurrence is in the twenty-first chapter of John, where he is simply named as one of the participants in the fishing expedition when Jesus appears to His disciples after His resurrection. It is in the previous episodes that John gives us an additional glimpse into his character.

The first mention of Thomas by John occurs in John 11, and is associated with the illness of Jesus' friend Lazarus, which historians date around A.D. 31-32. After Jesus had to leave Jerusalem due to the hostility of the Jewish leaders following His teaching that, "the Father and I are one"(John 10:30), Jesus knew, as well as His disciples, that the next time He set foot in Jerusalem they would attempt to put Him to death. Yet, a few months later, He received word that Lazarus, His great friend, was gravely ill. Jesus had often stayed in the home of Lazarus and his sisters, Mary and Martha, in nearby Bethany, right outside of Jerusalem. And although the message Jesus received was that Lazarus was very ill, Jesus told the Twelve, "This sickness is not unto death, but for the glory of God, that the Son of God may be glorified through it" (John 11:4). The disciples, no doubt, breathed a sigh of relief when Jesus uttered these words, thinking that He would no longer see the need to endanger Himself and the disciples by going to Bethany.

Yet the disciples had misunderstood His words, as His friend was in fact *already* dead. Jesus meant that Lazarus's death would not be the *ultimate* result of his sickness, knowing that He would glorify Himself by raising Lazarus from the dead. And so Jesus really brought confusion to the situation when John tells us that, although Jesus loved Martha and her sister and Lazarus, that when He heard of Lazarus's illness, "He stayed two more days in the place where He was" (John 11:5-6). A rather strange way to demonstrate one's love, wouldn't you say? But by Jesus' waiting two extra days, He made sure that Lazarus was dead. So by the time Jesus and His disciples had reached the burial place of Lazarus, he had been dead already four days (John 11:39).

One can easily understand how the disciples, then, became terrified when their Master announced His intention to go to Bethany, especially since it was probably too late to help Lazarus. The ministry in the wilderness had been very well received. Why go back to Bethany, near Jerusalem, within sight of the Temple? It is rarely pointed out that it was *only* Thomas who showed no reluctance to accompany Jesus to Bethany. Thomas challenged the other disciples, "Let us also go, that we may die with Him" (John 11:16). Clearly, Thomas's statement was both ironic and prophetic: ironic in that he did not grasp the uniqueness of Christ's impending death; and prophetic, in that his statement was an eerie prophecy intimating the martyrdom of all but one of the disciples. While all the apostles realized that not only their Master's life but their own lives would be put in jeopardy if they set foot near Jerusalem, it was only Thomas who was willing to put his life on the line for his Master. This passage clearly portrayed Thomas as a courageous and loyal disciple.

A second passage where Thomas is seen in detail occurs in the 14th chapter of John. This passage occurs in what is generally referred to as The Upper Room Discourse (John 13-17), where Jesus has turned aside to His disciples on the night in which He was betrayed to prepare them for His impending departure. The beginning of this chapter (commonly heard at funerals) speaks of Jesus telling the disciples that, "In my Father's house are many dwelling places; if it were no so, I would have told you so; for I go to prepare a place for you" (John 14:2). And after He tells them that He is going to prepare a place for them, and come again, and receive them, and "you know where I am going" (John 14:4), Thomas says to Him: "Lord, we do not know where You are going; *how* do we know the way?" (John 14:5). Thomas's words echo the words spoken by Peter just a few moments earlier in Jesus' meeting with His disciples, when Peter had said to Jesus, "Lord, where are you going?" (John 13:36), to which Jesus responded to Peter, "Where I go, you cannot follow Me now; but you shall follow later" (13:36). Jesus' response was an allusion to Peter's martyrdom in later years, following His Lord.

It surprises us to find that these words which have become familiar and comforting words of our Lord were obscure and puzzling to the apostles. They apparently were not persuaded that their Lord was shortly to die, so when He spoke of going to His "Father's house," it seemed incomprehensible to them that He was referring to His death, and going to be with His heavenly Father.

It is evident from this passage that Thomas has a deep and abiding love for the Lord. He doesn't want their Master to desert them, and yet he is totally bewildered by His statement. Thomas, often considered to be the mouthpiece for the despondency of the Twelve, speaks candidly of his confusion. It had to be a frightening time for Thomas and the rest of the disciples, as Christ prepares them for His departure, and He has just predicted that Peter would deny Him, despite his protests of allegiance! (John 14: 37-38) One gets a sense that there is a lot of confusion and fear among the disciples as they heard of His impending departure. They had grown to love Him over the past eighteen months of His earthly ministry, and one senses a deep love and affection that these men had for Jesus. It is as if you can hear Thomas' emotional lament and bewilderment that He is leaving them, but will come back for them: "Lord, we don't even know the *destination* of where you are headed, how in the world can we know the *way*?" This interruption by Thomas gives occasion for Jesus' famous declaration, "I am the Way, and the Truth, and the Life; no one comes to the Father, but through Me" (John 14:6).

While we get a picture of Thomas' *bravery* in John 11, and his *bewilderment* in John 14, it is the last vignette of Thomas, in John 20, for which he is best known to the world. After Jesus' death by crucifixion, the disciples are gathered in the Upper Room in Jerusalem on Sunday evening, to comfort one another over their deep sorrow of Christ's death (see Luke 24:36-43, and John 20:19-25). All except for Thomas, "called the Twin, who was not with them" (John 20:24). It was at this time, when the disciples had gathered on that first Sunday evening, with the doors shut due to their fear of the Jews (John 20:19), that Jesus came and stood in their midst, and said to them, "Peace be with you," and when He had said this, He showed them both His hands and His side. The disciples therefore rejoiced when they saw the Lord (John 20:19-20).

So where was Thomas when Christ showed Himself to the disciples on that first Easter Sunday evening? It may very well be that Thomas was so devastated and crushed after Christ's death that he simply couldn't stand the thought of even being with the other disciples. He most likely was off by himself wallowing in his own misery, regretting that he had not died along with his Master. He wasn't in a mood to be in a crowd, even with his fellow disciples who were his friends. So when the band of disciples later reported to Thomas, "We have seen the Lord!" (John 20:25), we can understand how he was in no mood to be taken in by such a fanciful idea. He had to be saying to himself, "Have these guys been dreaming? Don't you know dead men aren't raised from the dead?" So fittingly, he declares, "Unless I shall see in His hands the imprint of the nails, and put my finger into the place of the nails, and put my hand into His side, I will not believe" (John 20:25).

It is for this declaration of supposed "unbelief" that Thomas has been nicknamed, "Doubting Thomas." But if we consider other passages of the New Testament, it becomes clear that Thomas wasn't the ONLY disciple to disbelieve in the resurrection. Actually, Thomas had good company! Mark tells us in his Gospel that after Mary Magdalene saw Christ (His first resurrection appearance) and went to tell the other disciples that she had seen Him, "when they heard that He was alive, and had been seen by her, they refused to believe it" (Mark 16:11). Similarly, the two disciples that Jesus accompanied on the road to Emmaus on that first Sunday afternoon did not recognize Him for some time, until their eyes were opened after they reclined at table. They, too, were despondent, and were rebuked by Jesus for their unbelief, as He said to them: "O foolish men and slow of heart to believe in all that the prophets have spoken!" (Luke 24:25). Even the disciples who had gathered in the Upper Room did not believe the testimony of these two travelers on the road to Emmaus until Jesus Himself appeared to them, and showed them His hands and side (Mark 16:13, John 20:20).

It is not until a week later (John 20:26), when the disciples are gathered again in the room where Jesus had previously appeared to them, that Thomas is now with them, and Jesus again appeared to them, "the doors having been shut, and He stood in their midst, and said, 'Peace be with you'"(John 20:26). No one needed to tell Jesus what Thomas had said, but He simply offers the invitation to Thomas, "Reach here your finger, and see My hands; and reach here your hand, and put it into My side; and be not unbelieving, but believing." Thomas answered Him, "My Lord and my God!"(John 20: 27-28). What follows is Jesus' pronouncement, "Because you have seen Me, have you believed? Blessed are they who did not see, and yet believed" (John 20:29).

While Thomas is commonly referred to as the Doubter, due in large part to this passage in John 20, in reality *all* the disciples were slow to believe. Perhaps what set Thomas apart from the rest of the disciples was his initial grief, despondency, and bewilderment after the Lord's death, and his wish not to be in the company of the rest of the disciples. And while his desire to have "equal proof" as the other disciples seems a bit obstinate and unreasonable (with a shade of vanity), not willing to heed the testimony of the other disciples, it is also true that he was present with that little band of disciples on the *second* Lord's Day. Perhaps he was not so unbelieving as he at first seemed. Certainly he was not afraid of being convinced that His Lord had risen. And he had to realize the tremendous importance to him of this question—knowing that it was literally everything in the world if Christ was risen, and was now alive. So he kept in the company of believers.

While some might take Jesus' words of "challenge" to Thomas as harsh because he did not initially believe the report of the His being alive, the Lord was actually quite gentle with Thomas. Thomas wanted to see "living proof," and Jesus met him on his own terms. Jesus was tender with him, because, as the writer to the Hebrews observes, "He understands our doubts, weaknesses, and uncertainties about faith" (Hebrews 4:15). Marcus Dods, in his commentary on the Fourth Gospel discusses Thomas, and the issue of his unbelief:

*It was on their side he (Thomas) wished to get out of the terrible mire and darkness in which he was involved. It is this which distinguishes Thomas and all right-minded doubters from thorough-going and depraved unbelievers. The one wishes to believe, would give the world to be free from doubt, will go mourning all his days, will pine in body and sicken of life because he cannot believe: 'he waits for light, but behold obscurity, for brightness, but he walks in darkness.' The other, the culpable unbeliever, thrives on doubt; he likes it, enjoys it, sports it, lives by it; goes about telling people his difficulties, as some morbid people have a fancy for showing you their sores or detailing their symptoms, as if everything which makes them different from other men, even though it be disease, were a thing to be proud of. Convince such a man of the truth and he is as angry with you; you seem to have done him a wrong…You may know a dishonest doubter by the fluency with which he states his difficulties or by the affectation of melancholy which is sometimes assumed…When you find a man reading one side of the question, courting difficulties, eagerly seizing on new objections, and provoked instead of thankful when any doubt is removed, you may be sure that this is not a skepticism of the understanding so much as an evil heart of unbelief.*

But when we consider the faith of Thomas, it strengthens our own faith to hear such a decisive and full confession coming from the lips of such a man. John, the author of this Gospel, himself sensed something of the decisiveness of Thomas' confession, since he virtually closes his Gospel after recording his confession. You may recall that John tells us that the primary reason he has recorded this Gospel is to persuade men that Jesus is the Son of God (John 20:30-31). After Thomas' confession, hardly anything more needs to be said. One who is not moved by Thomas' confession will hardly be moved by any further proof. Proof is not what such a doubter needs, and whatever we may think of the other disciples, it is evident that Thomas at least was not credulous.

As stated at the outset, traditions suggest that Thomas carried the Gospel as far as India, and some suggest that he was martyred by being run through with a spear, probably around A.D. 72. How fitting a martyrdom for one whose faith was given evidence when he was shown the spear mark in his Lord's side, and for one who wanted to be reunited with his Lord.

Jesus didn't condemn Thomas, but met him where he was, and in our day, Jesus meets us amidst our own doubts and questions. Before we question the sincerity of those who may have doubts and questions; remember that doubts can become a means to a deeper, more vibrant faith, like it was for Thomas. As the writer Frederick Buechner has noted, "Whether your faith is that there is a God or that there is not a God, if you don't have any doubts you are either kidding yourself or asleep. Doubts are the ants in the pants of faith. They keep it awake and moving."

# DISCUSSION

*THE MANY FACES OF FAITH*

Despite being referred to as "Doubting Thomas" in the annals of church history, we get a glimpse of very different expressions of Thomas' faith in the New Testament. In John 11, as Jesus contemplates going back to Judea at the news of the illness of His good friend, Lazarus, in spite of the danger of the Jews, Thomas challenges his fellow disciples: "Let us also go, that we may die with Him!" (John 11:16).  How do you understand Thomas' words? What was he saying?

Later in the Gospel of John as Jesus prepares His disciples for His departure, Thomas remarks, "Lord, we don't know where you are going, so how can we know the way?" (John 14:6)

How are we to explain such different expressions of faith by Thomas between these two passages in John 11 and John 14?

Are such diverse expressions of faith the exception or the norm in terms of how people live their lives?

Why or why not?

*PROOF DEMANDED*

In John 20, after Jesus had already appeared to the disciples when Thomas was not present with them, and having been told that they had seen the risen Lord, Thomas exclaimed, "Unless I see the nail marks in His hands and put my finger where the nails were, and put my hand into His side, I will not believe it!" (John 20:25). Was Thomas demanding too much proof in order to believe?

Why or why not?

*MEETING HIM WHERE HE WAS*

A week later, when Jesus appeared to His disciples again after His resurrection, with all of the disciples present, including Thomas, He said to Thomas: "Put your finger here; see my hands. Reach out your hand and put it into my side. Stop doubting and believe" (John 20:27).What do you make of Jesus' words to him?

Do you think He was being too harsh on Thomas?

Why or why not?

## IS IT WRONG TO HAVE DOUBTS?

Is it wrong for us to have doubts about God, about His existence or goodness?

Take a look at Psalm 73, which is a recounting by the psalmist Asaph of his experience with questionings and doubts about God. What were the causes of his doubts?

What happened that allowed him to begin to get resolution with his questionings?

## DRILLING DOWN DEEP WHEN IT COMES TO DOUBTS

When people have doubts about God, is it simply because they don't believe His Word?

What else might lead to doubts and questions?

How should we respond to others who have serious doubts about God's existence, His goodness?

## BEING HONEST WITH GOD ABOUT DOUBTS

Have you ever had doubts about God, His existence, His goodness or His sovereignty?

If so, what led you to have these questions?

If your doubts have been resolved, what was the key to your resolving these issues?

If doubts about God still linger, how are you dealing with it?

# EXPRESSION

*"We both believe, and disbelieve a hundred times an Hour, which keeps Believing nimble."*

–Emily Dickinson

*"Whether your faith is that there is a God or that there is not a God, if you don't have any doubts you are either kidding yourself or asleep. Doubts are the ants in the pants of faith. They keep it awake and moving."*

–Frederick Buechner

*"Does God then forsake just those who serve Him best? Well, He who served Him best of all said, near His tortured death, 'Why hast thou forsaken me?' When God becomes man, that Man, of all others, is least comforted by God, at His greatest need. There is a mystery here which, even if I had the power, I might not have the courage to explore. Meanwhile, little people like you and me, if our prayers are sometimes granted, beyond all hope and probability, had better not draw hasty conclusions to our own advantage. If we were stronger, we might be less tenderly treated. If we were braver, we might be sent, with far less help, to defend far more desperate posts in the great battle."*

–C. S. Lewis, "The Efficacy of Prayer," *The World's Last Night and Other Essays*

*"I want to tell you something about me that you may see as weakness. I need wonder. I know that death is coming. I smell it in the wind, read it in the paper, watch it on television, and see it on the faces of the old. I need wonder to explain what is going to happen to me, what is going to happen to us when this thing is done, when our shift is over and our kids' kids are still on the earth listening to their crazy rap music. I need something mysterious to happen after I die. I need to be somewhere else after I die, somewhere with God, somewhere that wouldn't make any sense if it were explained to me right now. At the end of the day, when I am lying in bed…I need to know that God has things figured out, that if my math is wrong we are still going to be okay. And wonder is that feeling we get when we let go of our silly answers, our mapped out rules that we want God to follow. I don't think there is any better worship than wonder."*

–Donald Miller, *Blue Like Jazz: Nonreligious Thoughts on Christian Spirituality*

## MEDITATIONS

*"Surely God is good to Israel, to those who are pure in heart. But as for me, my feet had almost slipped; I had nearly lost my foothold. For I envied the arrogant when I saw the prosperity of the wicked…Surely in vain I have kept my heart pure; in vain have I washed my hands in innocence. All day long I have been punished every morning. If I had said, 'I will speak thus,' I would have betrayed your children. When I tried to understand all this, it was oppressive to me till I entered the sanctuary of God; then I understood their final destiny."*

–Psalm 73:1-3, 13-17

*"Therefore, since we have a great high priest who has gone through the heavens, Jesus the Son of God, let us hold firmly to the faith we profess. For we do not have a high priest who is unable to sympathize with our weaknesses, but we have one who has been tempted in every way, just as we are—yet was without sin. Let us then approach the throne of grace with confidence, so that we may receive mercy and find grace to help us in our time of need."*

–Hebrews 4:14-16

## REFLECTIONS

MAY I ALWAYS BE GRATEFUL…that the security of God's love is not jeopardized by my doubts and questionings, but is sure, as seen in Christ's giving His life for my sins.

MAY I ALWAYS BE MINDFUL…that there will be trials and challenges to my faith that I will not always understand.

MAY I ALWAYS BE HOPEFUL…that despite the doubts and trials that I have in life, God will meet me where I am, and ultimately bring me Home.

## Judas Iscariot
*No King to Me*
### The Mystery of Evil

For some two thousand years, the name "Judas" has carried an infamous ring to it, universally scorned as the betrayer of the Son of God. Every mention of him in the Scriptures alludes to his being a traitor, and his name appears last in every list of the disciples except for Luke's account in Acts 1, where he is not even mentioned. It is really difficult to fathom this most horrible of all deeds in human history, his betraying the perfect, sinless, holy Son of God for a paltry amount of money.

While the other disciples, despite their frailties, generally present us with models of hope, bravery, and encouragement, with Judas we are confronted with the reality of the darkness that resides in the human heart. We are reminded that people, even when they are surrounded by the Good, the True, and the Perfect, still can choose Evil. Here was a man who, despite having spent three years with Jesus in such a privileged position, still pursued his own devilish ends.

The New Testament tells us a good deal about Judas Iscariot. We know that his father's name was Simon (John 6:71). His name, *Judas*, is a Hellenized form of Judah, which is derived from the Hebrew root word, *yadah*, which means "to praise" (Genesis 49:8). How his parents must have had high hopes for their son to bring praise and thanksgiving to God! His surname, *Iscariot*, while uncertain, most likely signifies the region he came from, "man of Kerioth," which may be identified as Kerioth-Hezron (Joshua 15:25), an insignificant town in the south of Judea a few miles south of Hebron. Consequently, Judas is generally considered to be the only disciple from Judea, and not Galilee.

We also know that Judas' father was named Simon (John 13:2), but beyond this, in terms of his invitation from Jesus to be one of His disciples, we know nothing. He most likely was a young, zealous Jew, who desperately wanted to see the Roman rule overthrown, and had wagered that Christ would end the Roman oppression, and restore the kingdom to Israel. Like the other eleven disciples, he must have left whatever vocational endeavors he had to be a full-time follower of Christ. We do know that when many of the lukewarm followers of Christ deserted Him, because of Jesus' hard sayings, Judas remained faithful with the other Twelve (John 6:60ff.). Likewise, he must have shown himself to be a responsible disciple, because he ultimately attained a position of importance among the disciples, becoming the treasurer of the group, yet John tells us that he used his position to pilfer money (John 12:3-8, 13:29).

One of the most memorable episodes involving Judas occurred when Jesus and His disciples returned to the home of Mary, Martha, and Lazarus, whom He had raised from the dead (John 11). These good friends of Jesus lived in Bethany. Jesus was at the home of "Simon the Leper" (Matthew 26:6), being accompanied by His friend Lazarus, and his two sisters. John 12: 2-3 records the incident: "So they made Him a supper there; and Martha was serving; but Lazarus was one of those reclining at the table with Him. Mary therefore took a pound of very costly, genuine spikenard ointment, and anointed the feet of Jesus, and wiped His feet with her hair; and the house was filled with the fragrance of the ointment."

Needless to say, this was an extravagant show of worship and adoration, and had the appearance of wastefulness, and Judas was quick to point this out: "Why was this ointment not sold for three hundred *denarii* (about a year's wages), and given to the poor?" (John 12:5). Of course, in retrospect, John saw through Judas' clever ploy of concern for the poor: "Now he said this, not because he was concerned for the poor, but because he was a thief, and as he had the money box, he used to pilfer what was put into it" (John 12:6). Actually, Matthew, recounting this same event, observed that "all the disciples were indignant when they saw this, and said, 'What is the point of this waste?'" (Matthew 26:8). Jesus informs them, "Why do you bother the woman? For she had done a good deed to Me. For the poor you have with you always; but you do not always have Me" (Matthew 26:10-11).

Because of the Galilean disciples' unfamiliarity with Judas, this may have facilitated his ability to deceive the others of his intentions. And while he never seemed to have raised any suspicion among the disciples about his intentions (Matthew 26:22-23), Jesus knew Judas' heart, because He knows the heart of all men (John 2:24), and knew *from the beginning* Judas' intentions to betray Him (John 6:64). Although Christ knew that he would betray Him, it is also true that Christ had chosen him to be His disciple. Judas' decision to follow Jesus, and ultimately betray Him, is a mystery that challenges our finite understanding. Paradoxically, the Scriptures suggest that his betrayal was ordained, even prophesied, in the Old Testament. Several verses from various Psalms from the Old Testament, written by King David, while applying to himself, take on a more significant and ominous tone in the life of Christ:

*"For it is not an enemy who reproaches me, then I could bear it; nor is it one who hates me who has exalted himself against me, then I could hide myself from him. But it is you, a man my equal, my companion and my familiar friend. We who had sweet fellowship together, walked in the house of God in the throng" (Psalm 55:12-14).*

*"Even my close friend, in whom I trusted, who ate my bread, has lifted up his heel against me" (Psalm 41:9).*

The Scriptures suggest that following Judas' betrayal of Jesus by going to the chief priests (Mark 14:10f., 43-50), and having received the thirty pieces of silver, he felt remorse, and returned the money to the chief priests because he had "betrayed innocent blood" (Matthew 27:4). We read of his remorse and suicide in Matthew 27:3-10 and Acts 1:15-20. And because the priests could not keep the money that Judas returned, they bought the Potter's Field as a burial place for strangers (Matthew 27:7). In Matthew's account, he identifies another Old Testament passage, from the prophet Zechariah, as prophetically applying to Judas' actions:

*"They took the thirty pieces of silver, the price of the one whose price had been set by the sons of Israel; and they gave them for the Potter's Field, as the Lord directed me" (Zechariah 11:12-13).*

As difficult as it is to fathom, these Old Testament passages suggest that it was the designed plan of God for Judas to play the role of betrayer. And yet, Judas was never coerced into betraying Christ. He *willfully* carried out his betrayal – his own greed, ambition, and jealous desires – ultimately led to his treachery. and *yet,* God planned it in eternity past.

So how are we to reconcile the fact that Judas' betrayal was actually prophesied, along with the fact that he acted of his own accord? As problematic as this is, the Bible teaches that these seemingly contradictory "truths" are not contradictory, but rather to be held in tension, according to the foreordained plan of God. Jesus declared: "Behold, the hand of the one betraying Me is with Me on the table. For indeed, the Son of Man is going *as it has been determined*; but woe to that man through whom He is betrayed!" (Luke 22:21-22).

The apostle Peter addresses this issue of Christ's betrayal as part of God's sovereign plan in his sermon in the Book of Acts: "Men of Israel, listen to these words: Jesus the Nazarene, a man attested to you by God with miracles and wonders and signs which God performed through Him in your midst, just as you yourselves know–this Man, delivered up by the *predetermined plan* and foreknowledge of God, you nailed to a cross by the hands of godless men and put Him to death" (Acts 2:22-23).

Charles Haddon Spurgeon, the great nineteenth-century English preacher, helps us better reconcile the tension between God's sovereign plan and the matter of human choice:

*"If I find taught in one part of the Bible that everything is foreordained, that is true; and if I find, in another Scripture, that man is responsible for all his actions, that is true; and it is only my folly that leads me to imagine that these two truths can ever contradict each other. I do not believe they can ever be welded into one upon any earthly anvil, but they certainly shall be one in eternity. They are two lines that are so nearly parallel, that the human mind which pursues them farthest will never discover that they converge, but they do converge, and they will meet somewhere in eternity, close to the throne of God, whence all truth doth spring!"*

Sadly, Judas only knew of this *present* world, not a world to come, as offered by Jesus. When Jesus spoke to His disciples that in His kingdom "He who is greatest among you shall be your servant" (Matthew 23:11). This made little sense to the disciples, and especially not to a power-hungry Judas. Where is the victory when a man claiming to be the Promised King lays his power down? What legitimate King could think of reigning without a crown? Judas could not grasp the spiritual implications of the Eternal Kingdom Christ said that He had come to establish, a kingdom that would rule in the hearts of men forever. Judas could only believe in the worldly rule of man, a temporal world that, as the apostle Paul tells us, is *passing away* (1 Corinthians 7:31).

In his betrayal of Jesus Christ, Judas Iscariot stands out as one of the greatest tragedies in the annals of human history. His dark story is a poignant reminder, not only of the freedom of choice God gives to every human being, but also the depths of darkness that every soul is capable of reaching. Judas' life stands as a stark warning, as the Oxford don C.S. Lewis observed in his classic apologetic work, *Mere Christianity,* that the choices we make in life are making us more of a creature fit for either Heaven or Hell. Lewis writes: "every time you make a choice you are turning the central part of you, the part of you that chooses, into something a little different from what it was before…all your life long you are slowly turning this central thing either into a heavenly creature or into a hellish creature: either into a creature that is in harmony with God…or else into one that is in a state of war and hatred with God…Each of us at each moment is progressing to the one state or the other."

While all the other disciples (except John) would be martyred for their testimony concerning the Resurrected Christ, the Gospel of Matthew tells us of Judas' horrible fate after his betrayal of Jesus. Following his betrayal of Jesus, when he saw that Jesus had been condemned, he was filled with remorse and returned the thirty pieces of silver, throwing it into the temple and left, "and went away and hanged himself" (Matthew 27:5, cf. Acts 1:18).

While the other eleven disciples present us with models of bravery, hope, and encouragement, despite their frailties, with Judas we are confronted with the reality of the darkness that resides in the human heart. Sadly, Judas only could see life in terms of this present world, not a world to come as offered by Jesus. His dark story is a disturbing reminder of the freedom of choice God gives to every human soul, for either good or evil.

# DISCUSSION

*CONFRONTING THE UNEXPLAINABLE*

The betrayal of Jesus Christ by Judas Iscariot stands out as one of the most heinous acts in human history. How can we possibly understand that Jesus chose Judas to be one of His twelve disciples even though, as the Scriptures tell us (John 6:64), that he would betray Him?

*FORETOLD IN TIMES PAST*

Remarkably, there are a few Scriptures in the Old Testament that suggest Judas' betrayal was actually *foretold* centuries before it happened. Read Psalm 55:12-14, Psalm 41:9, and Zechariah 11:12-13. How do these passages speak to Judas' betrayal of the Son of God?

*GOD'S SOVEREIGNTY AND HUMAN CHOICE*

As difficult as it is to fathom, these Old Testament passages teach that it was the designed plan of God for Judas to play the role of the betrayer. Yet, the Scriptures never suggest that he was coerced into betraying Christ—he willingly carried out his betrayal. Read Luke 22:21-22 and Acts 2:22-23. How do these passages shed light on a very difficult subject?

How are we to understand the tension between the sovereign plan of God, and Judas' free will in betraying Jesus Christ?

*IS THERE REALLY EVIL IN OUR WORLD?*

On the night of His betrayal, as Jesus celebrated the Passover meal with His disciples, He said to His disciples, "He who shares my bread has lifted up his heel against Me (Psalm 41:9). I am telling you now before it happens, so that when it does happen you will believe that I am He" (John 13:18-19). When the disciples ask Jesus who it is who is betraying Him, Jesus responds: "It is the one to whom I will give this piece of bread when I have dipped it in the dish" (John 13:26). John then writes that immediately after Jesus gave the piece of bread to Judas Iscariot, "Satan entered into him. 'What you are about to do, do quickly,' Jesus told him" (John 13:27-28). What does this incident tell us about our world, and the reality of evil?

What do you think John means when he says that Satan *entered* Judas?

Do you think there is true evil in our world? Why or why not?

*A STRUGGLE NOT AGAINST FLESH AND BLOOD*

The Bible teaches that we are in a spiritual battle, and that "our struggle is not against flesh and blood" (Ephesians 6:12). What are some of the "instruments" for spiritual warfare that Paul mentions in Ephesians 6:10-18 that can help in our battle with temptation and evil?

Which do you think are the least "instruments" utilized in our battle with evil? Why?

*BACK TO THE GARDEN OF EDEN*

In the first book in the Bible, Genesis, chapter 3, we are told of Satan's temptation of Adam and Eve through the guise of a serpent in the Garden of Eden. How did he tempt them? What was his ploy in getting them to disobey God?

In what ways are the same strategies to tempt us present with us today?

How does Satan's temptation of Christ in the wilderness (Matthew 4:1-11, Luke 4:1-13) provide helpful insights into our own spiritual battle with evil and temptation?

# EXPRESSIONS

*"And do you now begin to see why Christianity has always said that the devil is a fallen angel? That is not a mere story for children. It is a real recognition of the fact that evil is a parasite, not an original thing... Enemy-occupied territory—that is what this world is. Christianity is the story of how the rightful king has landed, you might say landed in disguise, and is calling us all to take part in a great campaign of sabotage. When you go to church you are really listening-in to the secret wireless from our friends: that is why the enemy is so anxious to prevent us from going..."*

–C.S. Lewis, "The Invasion," *Mere Christianity*

*"Evil is unspectacular and always human,*
*And shares our bed and eats at our own table."*

–W.H. Auden, "Herman Melville"

*"Occasionally we talk of our Christianity as something that solves problems, and there is a sense in which it does. Long before it does so, however, it increases both the number and the intensity of the problems. Even our intellectual questions are increased by the acceptance of a strong religious faith...If a man wishes to avoid the disturbing effect of paradoxes, the best advice is for him to leave the Christian faith alone."*

–Elton Trueblood, *The Yoke of Christ*

## MEDITATIONS

*"What then? Shall we sin because we are not under law but under grace? By no means! Don't you know that when you offer yourselves to someone to obey him as slaves, you are slaves to the one whom you obey—whether you are slaves to sin, which leads to death, or to obedience, which leads to righteousness? But thanks be to God that, though you used to be slaves to sin, you wholeheartedly obeyed the form of teaching to which you were entrusted. You have been set free from sin and have become slaves to righteousness."*

–Romans 6:15-18

*"Finally, be strong in the Lord and in His mighty power. Put on the full armor of God so that you can take your stand against the devil's schemes. For our struggle is not against flesh and blood, but against the rulers, against the authorities, against the powers of this dark world and against the spiritual forces of evil in the heavenly realms."*

–Ephesians 6:10-12

## REFLECTIONS

MAY I ALWAYS BE GRATEFUL…that my God who dwells within me is greater than the evil one who is in the world.

MAY I ALWAYS BE MINDFUL…that this world, having been handed over to the Evil One, is a spiritual battleground.

MAY I ALWAYS BE HOPEFUL…that I will be strong in the Lord and in His mighty power, putting on the full armor of God, as I seek to be a follower of Jesus.

# Thaddaeus

*Reveal Yourself to Me*

**Hidden From the World, But Not From Those Who Seek Him**

The pages of the New Testament are virtually silent about the apostle Thaddaeus. What is interesting about him is that he had *three* names, leading Jerome, the Church Father, to refer to him as *Trionius*, the man with "three names." In Matthew 10:3, he is called "Lebbaeus, whose surname was Thaddaeus." In Mark 3:16-19, he is referred to as "Thaddaeus." And in the lists of the disciples found in Luke 6:14-16 and Acts 1:13, he is referred to as "Judas, the son of James." He very well may have been the son of James the Great, the son of Zebedee. And while the name Judas is a fine name in and of itself (meaning "Jehovah leads"), because of the negative association with Judas Iscariot, who betrayed Jesus, most prefer to call him Lebbaeus Thaddaeus. He was probably given the name Judas at birth, and Lebbaeus and Thaddaeus became essentially nicknames. The name "Thaddaeus" may be a diminutive of *Theudas* or *Theodore*, derived from the Aramaic noun *tad*, which means "breast," which would mean "dear" or "beloved." So this name, along with the other name, "Lebbaeus," (derived from the Hebrew noun, *Leb*, meaning, "heart") might suggest the meaning, "heart child," one close to the heart of the one who named him.

If his names to any extent fit his character, they suggest that he had a sensitive, tender heart. It seems strange that such a meek soul would be comfortable in the presence of the likes of some of the "thoroughbred" apostles like Peter, and the "Sons of Thunder," James and John!

We have only one incident in the New Testament where Thaddaeus is seen speaking among the disciples. In occurs in John's account of Jesus' Upper Room Discourse with the disciples on the night of His betrayal (John 13-17). In John 14, Jesus is preparing the disciples for His departure. As we read the chapter, we get the impression that the disciples didn't grasp the meaning of Jesus' words. After entertaining questions from Thomas and Phillip (John 14:5, 8), Jesus tells His disciples:

*"After a little while the world will no longer see Me, but you will see Me; because I live, you will live also. In that day you will know that I am in My Father, and you in Me, and I in you. He who has My commandments and keeps them is the one who loves Me; and he who loves Me will be loved by My Father, and I will love him and will disclose Myself to him" (John 14:19-21).*

If Jesus' earlier words to them were incomprehensible, He now tells them something even more difficult, that the world will no longer see Him, but they will see Him. Further, that if they keep His commandments, He will disclose Himself to them. Hard words. Profound words. John then records Thaddaeus' question to Jesus in verse 22: " Lord, what then has happened that You are going to disclose Yourself to us, and *not* to the world?'"

Thaddaeus was clearly asking Jesus a very penetrating question. If, after all, Jesus was the Savior of the world, the rightful Heir who was inaugurating His Messianic kingdom on earth, and subdue all things to Himself, why would He *not* want to disclose Himself to the whole world? Here was a sincere question from, on all accounts, a pious, tender-hearted follower. Thaddaeus really wanted to know: why was Jesus going to make Himself known to this ragamuffin group of disciples, and *not* to everyone in the world? In his mind he could not square this statement with his belief that the kingdom must arrive in undeniable and irresistible splendor. If Jesus is the Messianic King, then He *must* startle the world with apocalyptic self-disclosure (e.g. Isaiah 11, Daniel 7, Zechariah 9). But Jesus gives Thaddaeus, the rest of the disciples, and us as well, a remarkable answer, an answer that went far beyond the political, physical, and geographical boundaries of the Jewish world:

*"If anyone loves Me, he will keep My word; and My Father will love him, and We will come to him and make Our abode with him" (John 14:23).*

The word translated in verse 23, "abode" (Greek, *mone*, "home, dwelling place") only occurs in the New Testament one other time, and that is earlier in this same chapter, where Jesus tells the disciples: "In My Father's house are many *dwelling-places*; if it were not so, I would have told you; for I go to prepare a place for you" (John 14:2). While Jesus has told His disciples that He is leaving in order to prepare "dwelling-places" for His followers (John 14:2), He also simultaneously promises to join with the Father in making a "dwelling-place" in the believer. Jesus here promises His disciples that personal devotion to Christ, which leads to obedience to His word (John 14:23), will lead them to personally experience God (John 14:21, 23). Jesus was telling His disciples that He was not in the world to take over the world through brute, physical force, but rather through each individual heart that responds in faith and obedience to His word. He and the Father would come to that believer and set up the kingdom in their *heart*s.

And what became of Thaddaeus? Early church tradition suggests that he took the Gospel north to Edessa after Pentecost, a royal city of Mesopotamia (near modern day Turkey). There are also numerous accounts of how he supposedly healed the king of Edessa, a man named Abgar. The traditional apostolic symbol of Judas Lebbaeus Thaddaeus is a club, because some traditions suggest that he was clubbed to death because of his testimony for Christ.

With Thaddaeus, another unsung and obscure disciple, we are shown how God uses ordinary men and women to accomplish His purposes in the world. We are also reminded of how his question of Christ in the Upper Room, among all the other disciples, is a fitting promise that Jesus and His Heavenly Father will come and reveal Themselves to us—making Their *abode* with us—if we seek Him with all our hearts. Jesus was promising His disciples, and for those who seek Him today, that He and the Father would actually come and make their *abode*, their *dwelling place*, with that person. Is this not the great promise of the Bible? That the Creator of the universe, the Architect of all creation, promises, when we respond in faith, to come into our lives, and reveal Himself to us, and make His *abode* with us? Is this not the burning desire of the human heart—to know God, and to be known by God? For us to truly see, "Who You Are?"

*"Behold, I stand at the door and knock. If anyone hears My voice and opens the door, I will come in to him, and dine with him, and he with Me." –*Revelation 3:20

# DISCUSSION

*A TENDERHEARTED FOLLOWER*

Thaddaeus may well have been the son of James the Great (Luke 16:14-16), one of the prominent disciples in Jesus' inner circle. If his nicknames Labbaeus and Thaddaeus have any significance ("beloved child, tenderhearted one"), he may have been a sensitive, tender man, not likely at ease with the likes of a Peter, or one of the Sons of Thunder, James or John! Why do you think Jesus might have chosen such a timid and sensitive follower to be one of His twelve disciples?

How does the Apostle Paul's choosing of another young tenderhearted man, Timothy, for his unrivaled leadership (Philippians 2:19-22) possibly mirror Jesus' selection of a Thaddaeus?

How do these passages give us some insight into what Timothy was like? 1 Corinthians 16:10-11, and 2 Timothy 1:6-7.

*CHRIST HIDDEN FROM THE WORLD*

Jesus tells His disciples: "Before long, the world will not see Me anymore, but you will see Me. Because I live, you also will live" (John 14:19). Jesus' statement leads to Thaddaeus' question of Jesus: "But Lord, why do you intend to show yourself to us and not to the world?" (John 14:22) It was incomprehensible to Thaddaeus that Christ would reveal Himself to His disciples, and not to the whole world! Why would Christ choose not to reveal Himself to the world in His irresistible splendor?

Why do you think God has not chosen to always reveal Himself to the world in spectacular fashion?

What is the relationship between Jesus not revealing Himself to the world, and His Incarnation, when the Son of God became a man?

*GOD MAKING HIS HOME WITH US*

Jesus responds to Thaddaeus' question in verse 23: "If anyone loves Me, he will obey My teaching. My Father will love him, and we will come to him and make our *home* with him." The word "home" is a related word to the word "rooms" or "dwelling places" in John 14:2. What do you think is the connection between these two verses?

What is Jesus promising His followers?

How is our obedience to His Word related to the promise?

*EXPERIENCING GOD*

Can you think of a time when you felt or experienced the presence of God in your life?

If so, what were the circumstances that led up to this experience? Was it during good times or bad times?

Was your experiencing the presence and power of God in any way related to your obedience?

# EXPRESSIONS

*"My Lord God, I have no idea where I am going. I do not see the road ahead of me. I cannot know for certain where it will end. Nor do I really know myself, and the fact that I think I am following your will does not mean that I am actually doing so. But I believe that the desire to please you does in fact please you."*

–Thomas Merton, "Thoughts in Solitude"

*"If there were no obscurity man would not feel his corruption: if there were no light man could not hope for a cure. Thus it is not only right but useful for us that God should be partly concealed and partly revealed, since it is equally dangerous for man to know God without knowing his own wretchedness as to know his own wretchedness without knowing God."*

–Pascal, *Pensees*, #446

*"I find I must borrow yet another parable from George MacDonald. Imagine yourself as a living house. God comes in to rebuild that house. At first, perhaps, you can understand what He is doing. He is getting the drains right and stopping the leaks in the roof and so on: you knew that those jobs needed doing and so you are not surprised. But presently he starts knocking the house about in a way that hurts abominably and does not seem to make sense. What on earth is He up to? The explanation is that He is building quite a different house from the one you thought of—throwing out a new wing here, putting on an extra floor there, running up towers, making courtyards. You thought you were going to be made into a decent little cottage: but He is building a palace. He intends to come and live in it Himself."*

–C. S. Lewis, "Counting the Cost," *Mere Christianity*

# MEDITATIONS

*"The knowledge of the secrets of the kingdom of heaven has been given to you, but not to them. Whoever has will be given more, and he will have an abundance. Whoever does not have, even what he has will be taken from him. This is why I speak to them in parables: 'Though seeing, they do not see; though hearing, they do not hear or understand.'"*

–Matthew 13:11-13

*"Behold, I stand at the door and knock. If anyone hears My voice and opens the door, I will come in to him, and dine with him, and he with Me."*

–Revelation 3:20

# REFLECTIONS

MAY I ALWAYS BE GRATEFUL…that God has come into my life to take up residence with me, and will never leave me.

MAY I ALWAYS BE MINDFUL…that obedience plays a part in God revealing Himself to me, and His plan for our lives.

MAY I ALWAYS BE HOPEFUL…that God will reveal Himself to me in greater ways as I seek to obey Him and His Word.

# Andrew
## *Sea of Men*
### *Telling Others*

Although Andrew was the first disciple whom Jesus called, ironically, he is, among the lead disciples, the one we know the *least* about. Curiously, Andrew, Peter's brother, is not included in some of the significant events that the inner circle of Peter, James, and John experienced. He is nowhere to be found when Christ has these three disciples with Him at the Mount of Transfiguration, the healing of Jairus' daughter, and accompanying Him to pray in Gethsemane (Matthew 17:1, Mark 5:37, Mark 14:33). Apart from the places where all twelve disciples are listed, Andrew's name only appears in the New Testament nine times, and most of those occasions simply mention him in passing. Yet while Andrew wasn't featured as one of the inner circle, it is clear that he had a close relationship with Christ.

Andrew and his better-known sibling, Peter, the undisputed leader among the disciples, were originally from the village of Bethsaida in northern Galilee (John 1:44), which was about 25 miles east of Nazareth, situated on the northern shore of the Sea of Galilee. Yet at some point it is evident that they relocated to the larger city of Capernaum, and shared a home there while operating their fishing business (Mark 1:29). It is quite possible that their home served as Jesus' primary residence during His ministry there. The two brothers were most likely lifelong companions with the sons of Zebedee, James and John, who were also from the Capernaum. It is also reasonable to believe that these four fishermen also had similar spiritual interests. They most likely were on a sabbatical break from their fishing when they first became disciples of John the Baptist in the wilderness, when they also first encountered Christ.

The apostle John tells us of his and Andrew's first meeting with Jesus, and records the encounter as an eyewitness. When John and Andrew were together the day after Jesus' baptism (John 1:29-34), as Jesus approached, John the Baptist proclaimed, "Behold, the Lamb of God." The two of them immediately left John the Baptist and began to follow Jesus (John 1:37).

John's account of what transpired continues, as he records how Jesus dealt with himself and his friend, Andrew: "Then Jesus turned, and seeing them following, said to them, 'What do you seek?' They said to Him, 'Rabbi (which is to say, when translated, Teacher), 'where are You staying?' He said to them, 'Come and see.' They came and saw where He was staying, and remained with Him that day" (John 1:38-39). It was late in the afternoon, about four o'clock in the afternoon ("the tenth hour," verse 39) when Andrew and John met Christ, and this afternoon spent in private conversation with Jesus convinced the two of them that they had found the true Messiah.

We learn something important about Andrew's character when we note the very first thing he did after spending time with Christ that day – "he first found his own brother Simon, and said to him, 'We have found the Messiah,' (which is translated, "the Christ"), and he brought him to Jesus" (John 1:41-42). While Andrew and Peter would return to Capernaum to continue their fishing operation after that initial meeting with Christ, it was probably a few months later that Jesus came to Galilee to begin His ministry there, when these brothers left their fishing business permanently to become a full-time disciples of Christ (Matthew 4:18-22, Luke 5:1-11).

While it is clear that Andrew labored in the shadow of his better-known brother, there is no evidence that he ever begrudged Peter's dominance in his leadership among the disciples. Indeed, Andrew is the one who brought Peter to Christ in the first place!

What is more, it seems that almost every time we see Andrew mentioned in the Gospels, he is bringing *individuals* to Jesus. After he initially brought Peter to Christ (John 1:39ff.), we witness Andrew, at Christ's miraculous feeding of the five thousand, bringing the boy with the loaves and the fishes to Christ to see what He might do, "There is a lad here who has five barley loaves and two small fish" (John 6:9). Later in John's Gospel, there are a number of Greeks who, having heard of Jesus' reputation sought out Philip and asked to see Jesus. John writes that these men "came to Philip, who was from Bethsaida of Galilee, and asked him, saying, 'Sir, we wish to see Jesus.' Philip came and told Andrew, and in turn Andrew and Philip told Jesus" (John 12:20-22).

The Bible does not tell us what happened to Andrew after the birth of the church at Pentecost (Acts 2). Tradition suggests he carried the Gospel north, and Eusebius, the early church historian, says Andrew went as far as Scythia, which is southern Russia around the area of the Black Sea. This is why Andrew is considered the patron saint of Russia (he is also the patron saint of Scotland). Several other strong traditions place his ministry in Ephesus and Asia Minor, to be with his old friend, the apostle John. Still another tradition places his ministry in Greece, where he was imprisoned by the proconsul/governor, Aegeates, because his wife Maximilla had been converted through his preaching.

Tradition also suggests that Andrew was ultimately crucified in Achaia, which is located in the southern portion of Greece, near Athens, around A.D. 69. Supposedly, Andrew was crucified, not upon a traditional cross as the one Christ was crucified on, but rather a cross made in the shape of an "X." To this day, this kind of cross is referred to as St. Andrew's cross.

And what was Andrew's legacy? As far as we know, Andrew never preached to multitudes or founded any churches. Neither did he write an epistle. Luke the physician, who chronicled the events of the early church, never even mentions Andrew in his work, the Acts of the Apostles. Yet, in many ways, Andrew serves as a worthy model for all who labor quietly in humble, unsung places. He saw the eternal value, not in the crowds and the hoopla, but in introducing *individuals* to Christ. That simple invitation from Christ to become a "fisher of men" was an invitation that deep inside, he knew he had to follow. Having abandoned all he once called "mine," Andrew knew he must heed the Master's call to cast his nets, now over a sea of men.

And that simple invitation of Jesus to become a "fisher of men" is addressed to you and me today. As God gives us the opportunity to introduce people to Jesus, we sense His eternal purpose and design for our lives. So many people are waiting, waiting to be gathered into the Kingdom of God. Will we heed the call of Jesus in our lives?

# DISCUSSION

*ON THE OUTSIDE LOOKING IN*

Andrew, as the brother of the undisputed leader of the Twelve, Peter, is not included in some of the most significant events that the inner circle of disciples (Peter, James and John) took part in with Jesus. What do you think went through his mind when he wasn't included with his brother and James and John, who were probably his closest friends?

Have you ever found yourself in a similar situation, where you felt unappreciated or jealous of others success or being included?

How did you handle it?

How do you think God wants us to respond to such situations?

*BRINGING PEOPLE TO MEET JESUS*

It is curious to note that almost every time we see Andrew mentioned in the Gospels, he is bringing people to meet Jesus! Read John 1:39ff., John 6:7ff, and John 12:20-22. As you read these three passages, what comes to mind about Andrew's personality?

What would you say his giftedness may have been?

Do you enjoy telling others about Christ and your Christian faith? Why or why not?

*CONTENTMENT WITH GOD'S PLAN*

Despite being in the first group disciples, along with his brother Peter and the sons of Zebedee, we know the *least* about Andrew. And even though he and the disciple John were the first to meet and talk with Jesus (John 1:35ff.), Andrew tends to fade into the background. Do you think Andrew was ever jealous of his brother Peter's prominence among the disciples?

Why or why not?

How does Andrew's life and legacy serve as a worthy model for us to follow?

What does it say about contentment with where God has placed us in life?

Are we content with His plan for our lives?

"There is a dread code word that church people, particularly Professional Church People, use for those who are, well, un-churched. For sheer stupidity it ranks with 'deplane,' as in 'in an emergency, you will deplane from the door or window nearest you that is marked as an exit.' My favorite days are those in which I am a thoroughly 'deplaned' person. The best commentary on the word 'unchurched' that I know of came from a grocer in a small town in Iowa, apparently one of the suspect heathen. One day the pastor of the Lutheran church approached him about providing food for a district meeting on church evangelization committees. These are the people, the pastor explained, who have a special ministry— here he paused, significantly—a special outreach to the 'unchurched.' The grocer took the order for cold cuts, sliced cheeses, rolls, cookies, and fruit. When the pastor unveiled the large deli platter in the church basement, he was startled to find that the centerpiece was a cross constructed out of slices of bologna."

–Kathleen Norris, *Amazing Grace*

"It is precisely because of the eternity outside time that everything in time becomes valuable and important and meaningful. Therefore, Christianity…makes it of urgent importance that everything we do here should be rightly related to what we eternally are. 'Eternal life' is the sole sanction for the values of this life."

–Dorothy L. Sayers

"Our life is a short time in expectation, a time in which sadness and joy kiss each other at every moment. There is a quality of sadness that pervades all the moments of our life. It seems that there is no clear-cut pure joy, but that even in the most happy moments of our existence we sense a tinge of sadness. In every satisfaction, there is an awareness of limitations. In every success, there is the fear of jealousy. Behind every smile, there is a tear. In every embrace, there is loneliness. In every friendship, distance. And in all forms of light, there is the knowledge of surrounding darkness…But this intimate experience in which every bit of life is touched by a bit of death can point us beyond the limits of our existence. It can do so by making us look forward in expectation to the day when our hearts will be filled with perfect joy, a joy that no one shall take away from us."

-Henri Nouwen, *Making All Things New*

## MEDITATIONS

*"Devote yourselves to prayer, being watchful and thankful. And pray for us, too, that God may open a door for our message, so that we may proclaim the mystery of Christ, for which I am in chains. Pray that I may proclaim it clearly, as I should. Be wise in the way you act toward outsiders; make the most of every opportunity. Let your conversation be always full of grace, seasoned with salt, so that you may know how to answer everyone."*

–Colossians 4:2-6

*"But godliness with contentment is great gain. For we brought nothing into the world, and we can take nothing out of it. But if we have food and clothing, we will be content with that. People who want to get rich fall into temptation and a trap and into many foolish and harmful desires that plunge men into ruin and destruction…"*

–1Timothy 6:6-9

## REFLECTIONS

MAY I ALWAYS BE GRATEFUL…for God's simple invitation in my life to follow Him.

MAY I ALWAYS BE MINDFUL…to be content with God's plan for my life.

MAY I ALWAYS BE HOPEFUL…that God would give me the privilege to tell others what it means to become a follower of Jesus Christ.

# About the Author

Barry Morrow brings over twenty years of experience of working in the marketplace with businessmen through writing, teaching, and consulting. He has served on the staff of Reflection's Ministries for the past eight years, and spent the previous fifteen years in pastoral ministry in a nondenominational church in suburban Atlanta. *FinishingWell*, a consulting and mentoring program for executives, serves under the auspices of Reflections Ministries, Inc., a non-profit organization that focuses on serving men in the workplace.

He received his undergraduate degree in Biology from the University of North Carolina at Chapel Hill. He later attended Dallas Theological Seminary, where he graduated with High Honors. At Dallas Seminary he received a Masters Degree in Semitics and Old Testament Exegesis, and was awarded the Jennie Solomon Award in Old Testament.

Barry's book, *Heaven Observed: Glimpses of Transcendence in Everyday Life*, was published by NavPress in 2001. The book examines our desire and quest for meaning, purpose, and happiness in life, and examines the various avenues through which we attempt to find such fulfillment, "signposts" to another world awaiting us. He and his wife, Caroleeta, reside in Roswell, Georgia, and are the parents of two children, Anna and Jonathan.

# What Others Are Saying

"Barry Morrow is an exceptional Bible teacher. For the last six years, I have had the opportunity to benefit from his teaching and ministry. I am happy and excited to commend his ministry *FinishingWell* with business professionals, for he not only has an excellent grasp of the Scriptures, but he also relates well to professional men, encouraging them to live out their Christian faith with passion and clarity."

-Horst H. Schulze
Founding President and COO, The Ritz-Carlton Hotel Company, LLC
President and CEO, The West Paces Hotel Group, LLC
Atlanta, Georgia

"Through *FinishingWell*, Barry Morrow brings a fresh and insightful perspective to men to assist them on their spiritual journey. Barry's focus is to help us discover our unique Kingdom calling and to maximize our potential in fulfilling that calling. I have had the opportunity to be directly involved in Barry's ministry and to benefit from his teaching, experience, and encouragement. He is exceptional in this environment."

-J. Allen Wright
Senior Vice President-Investments
PRIME Asset Consulting, UBS
Atlanta, Georgia

Barry L. Morrow
Reflections Ministries, Inc.
One Piedmont Center, Suite 130
Atlanta, Georgia 30305
Website: Finishingwell.com
Phone: 404.513.0404
Email: bmorrow@finishingwell.com